MINDWORKS ART Volume 3
a spiritual journey

by Richard Fisher

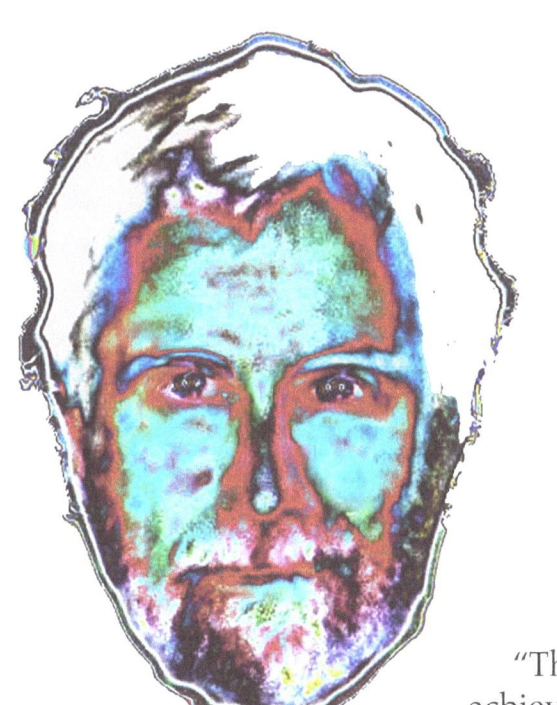

"The face is an artistic
achievement. The face is the
mirror of the mind.
If we become addicted to
the external, our interiority
will haunt us."
~JOHN O'DONOHUE,
Anam Cara,
a Book of Celtic Wisdom, 1997

Website: http://www.MINDWORKSart.com
Email: richardfisher@mindworksart.com

Title ID: 5158707
ISBN-13: 978-1505436426

Printed by CreateSpace.com

Front Cover: *Oz Head*

The origin of this image is
a photo of my head which
was modified in
Photoshop program with
filters called Kai's Power
Tools, Video Cyclone,
which morphs colors in
endless combinations.

Back Cover: *The Flowering of
Human Consciousness*

"...dis-identify from your thoughts and
experience the shift in identity from
being the content of your mind to being
the awareness in the background."
~ECKHART TOLLE, *A New Earth*, 2005

Introduction

What are MINDWORKS?

MINDWORKS are drawing meditations, images rising from the unconscious mind...a process of discovery, art put to the service of self-realization for the artist as well as the viewer.

> "A human being is part of the whole, called by us 'Universe'; a part limited in time and space. He experiences himself, his thoughts and feelings, as something separated from the rest--a kind of optical delusion of his consciousness.
>
> This delusion is a kind of prison for us, restricting us to our personal desires and affection for a few persons nearest us. Our task must be to free ourselves from this prison by widening our circle of compassion to embrace all living creatures and the whole of nature in its beauty.
>
> Nobody is able to achieve this completely but striving for such achievement is, in itself, a part of the liberation and a foundation for inner security."
>
> ~**Albert Einstein** as quoted in *Quantum Reality: Beyond the New Physics* by Nick Herbert

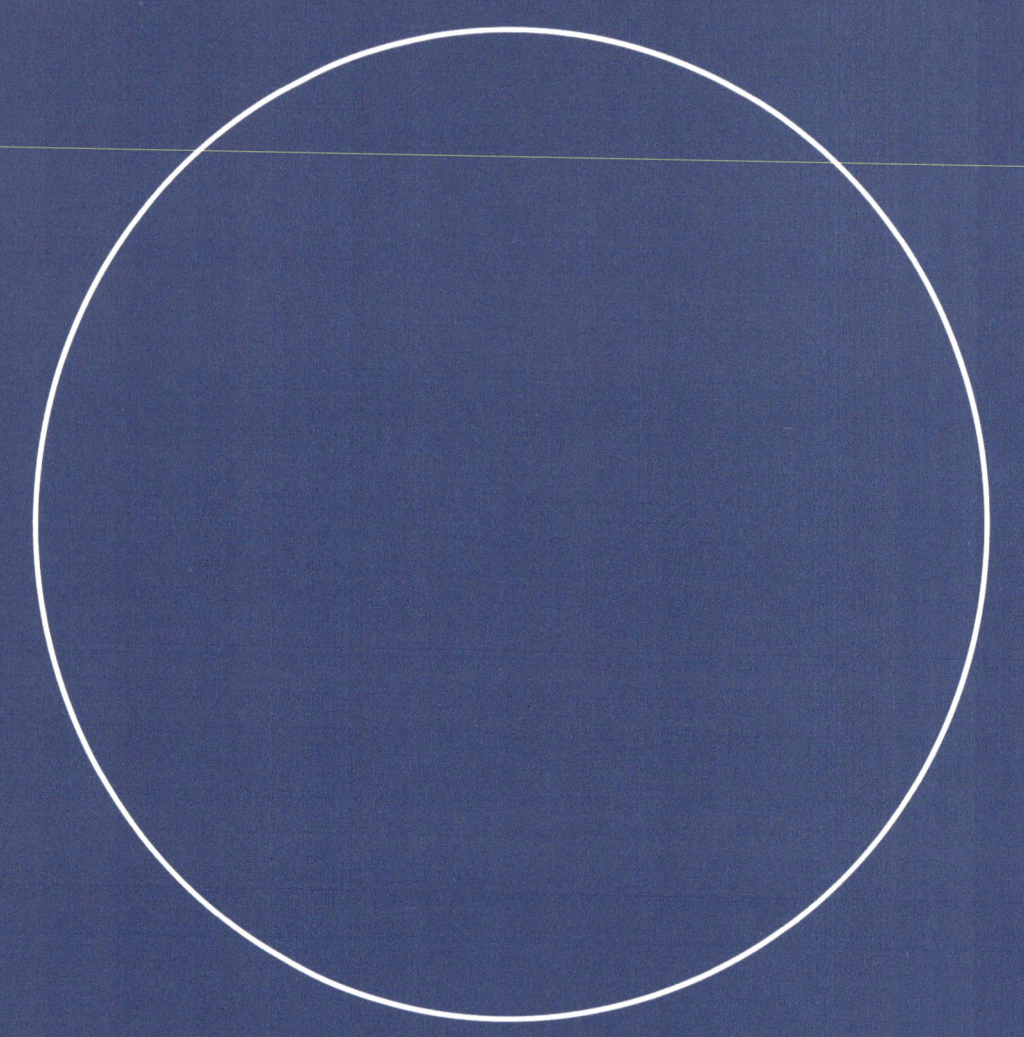

"The imagination is a great friend of the
unknown. Endlessly, it invokes and
releases the power of possibility."
~JOHN O'DONOHUE, *Anam Cara,*
a Book of Celtic Wisdom, 1997

Right:
Interior of a pot,
a very ordinary pot.

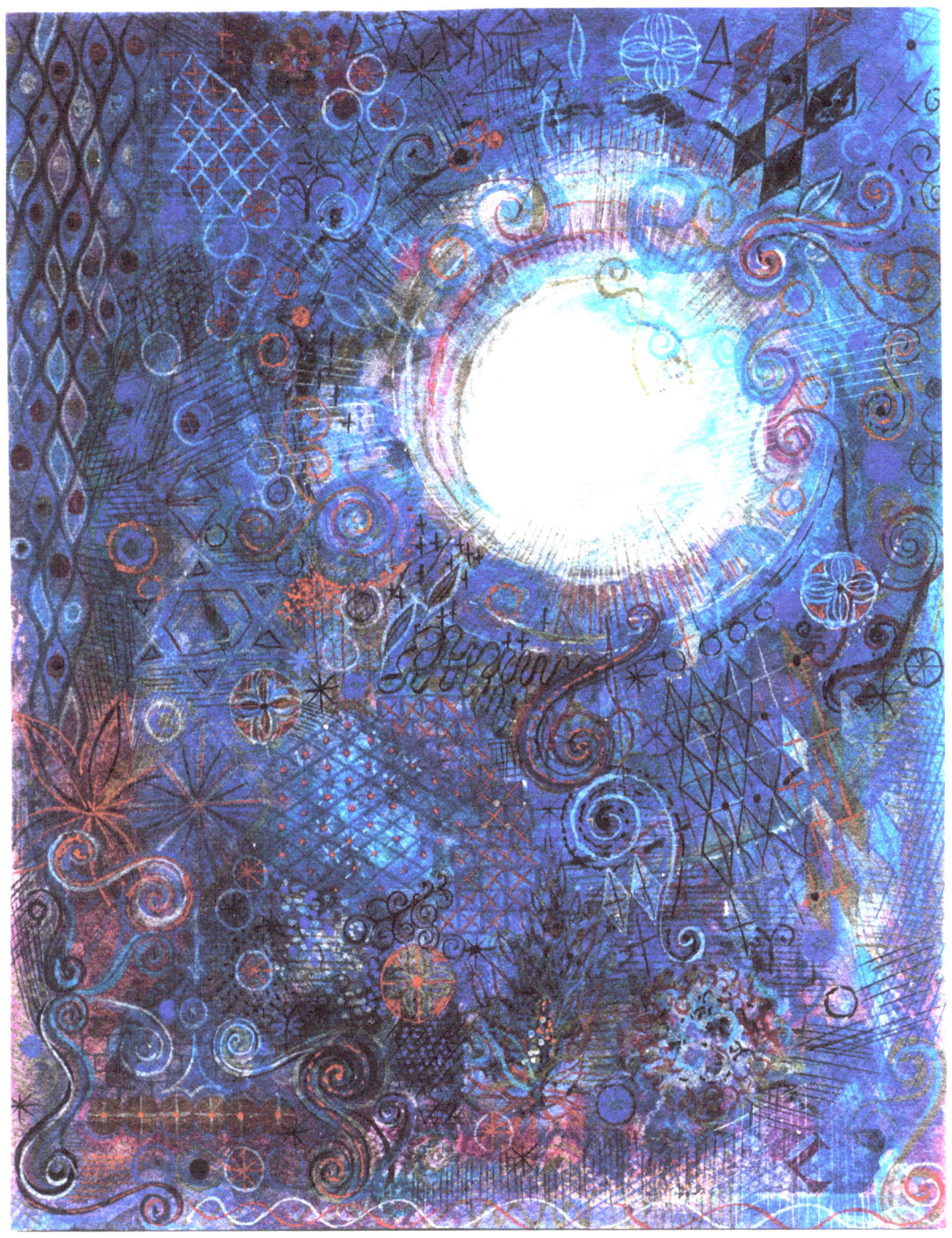

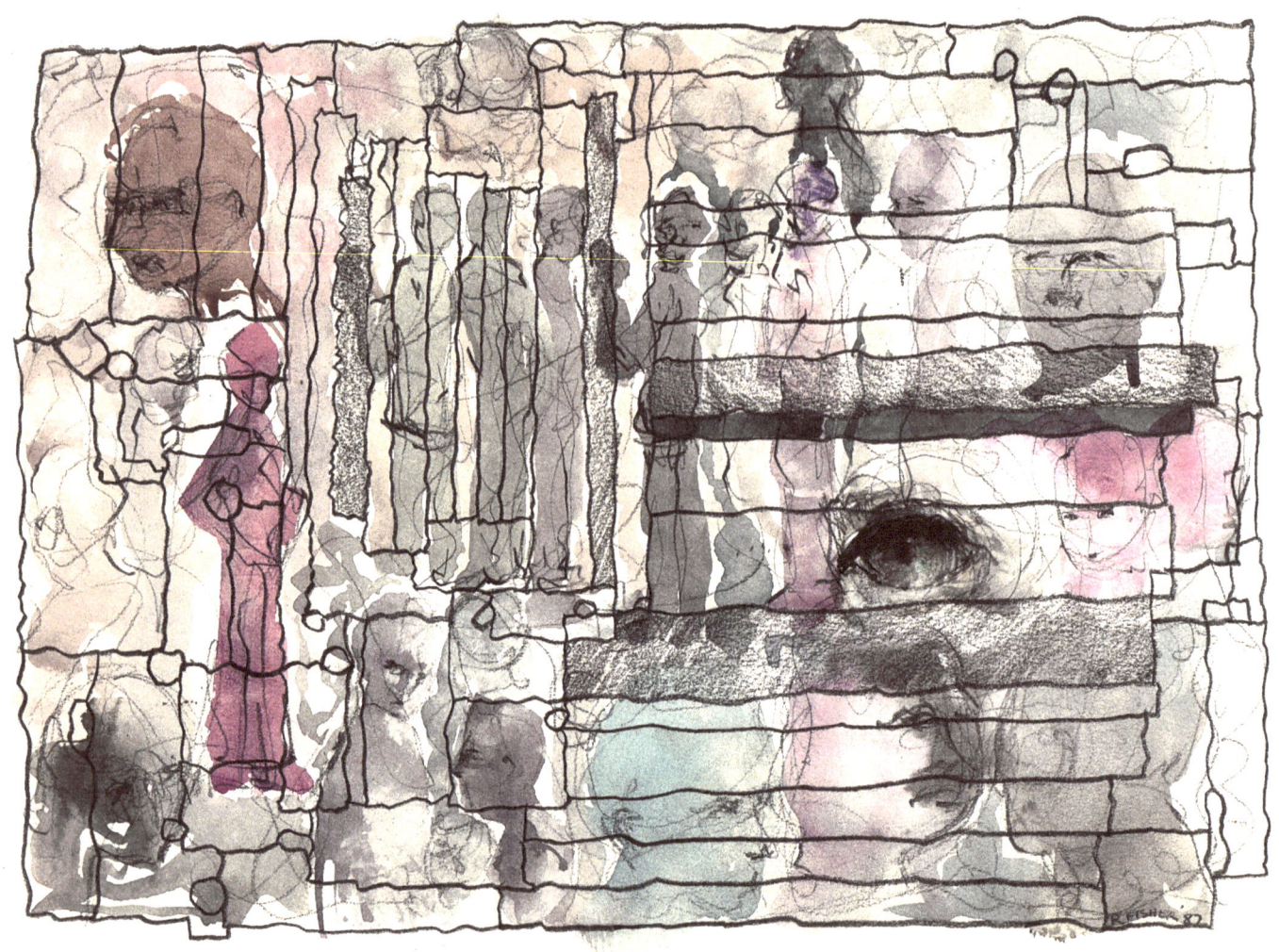

MindGate

"We already are channels of creative energy.
The challenge seems to be for us to accept
that gift and develop its expression."
~HENRY REED, *Edgar Cayce on Channeling Your
Higher Self,* 1989

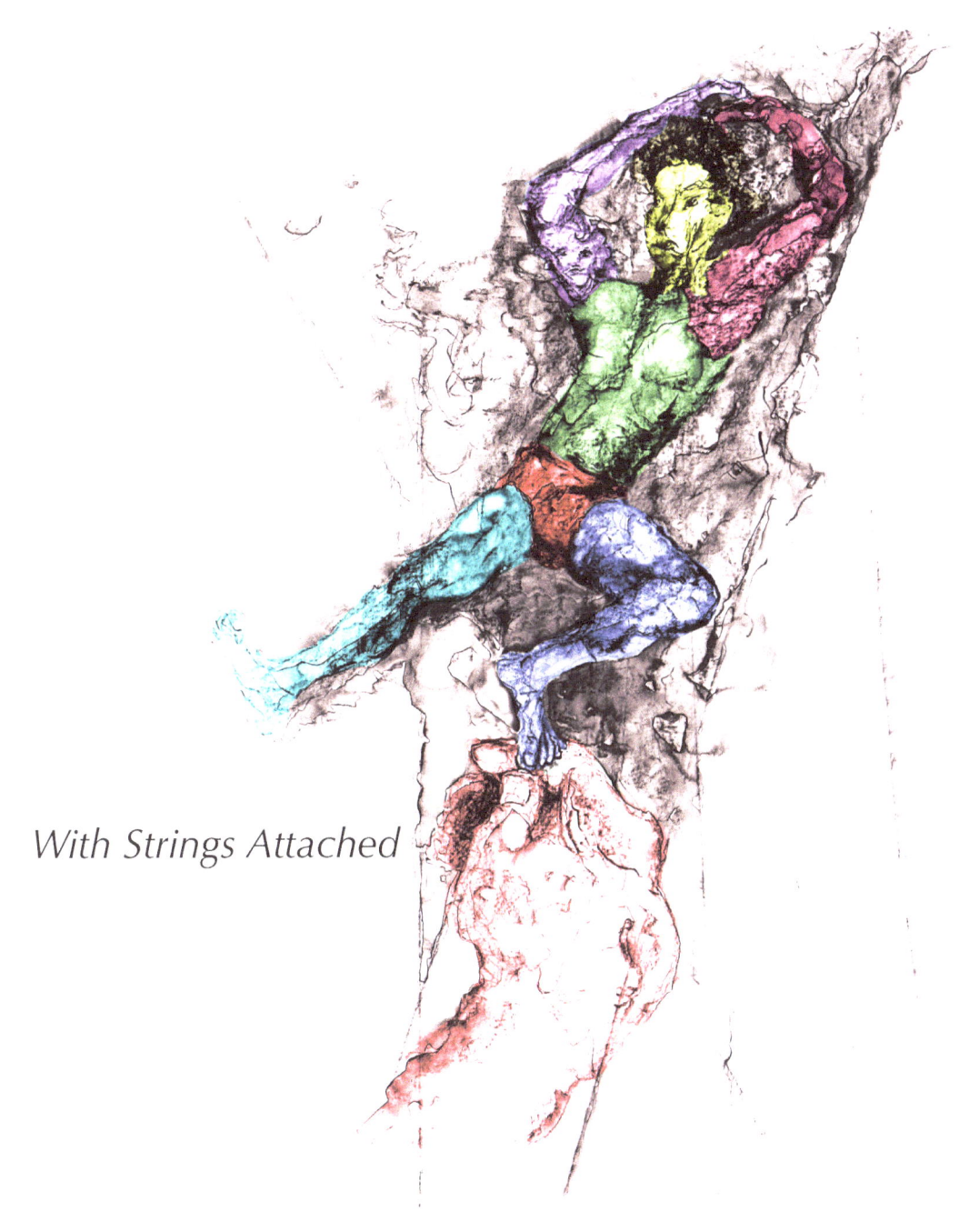

With Strings Attached

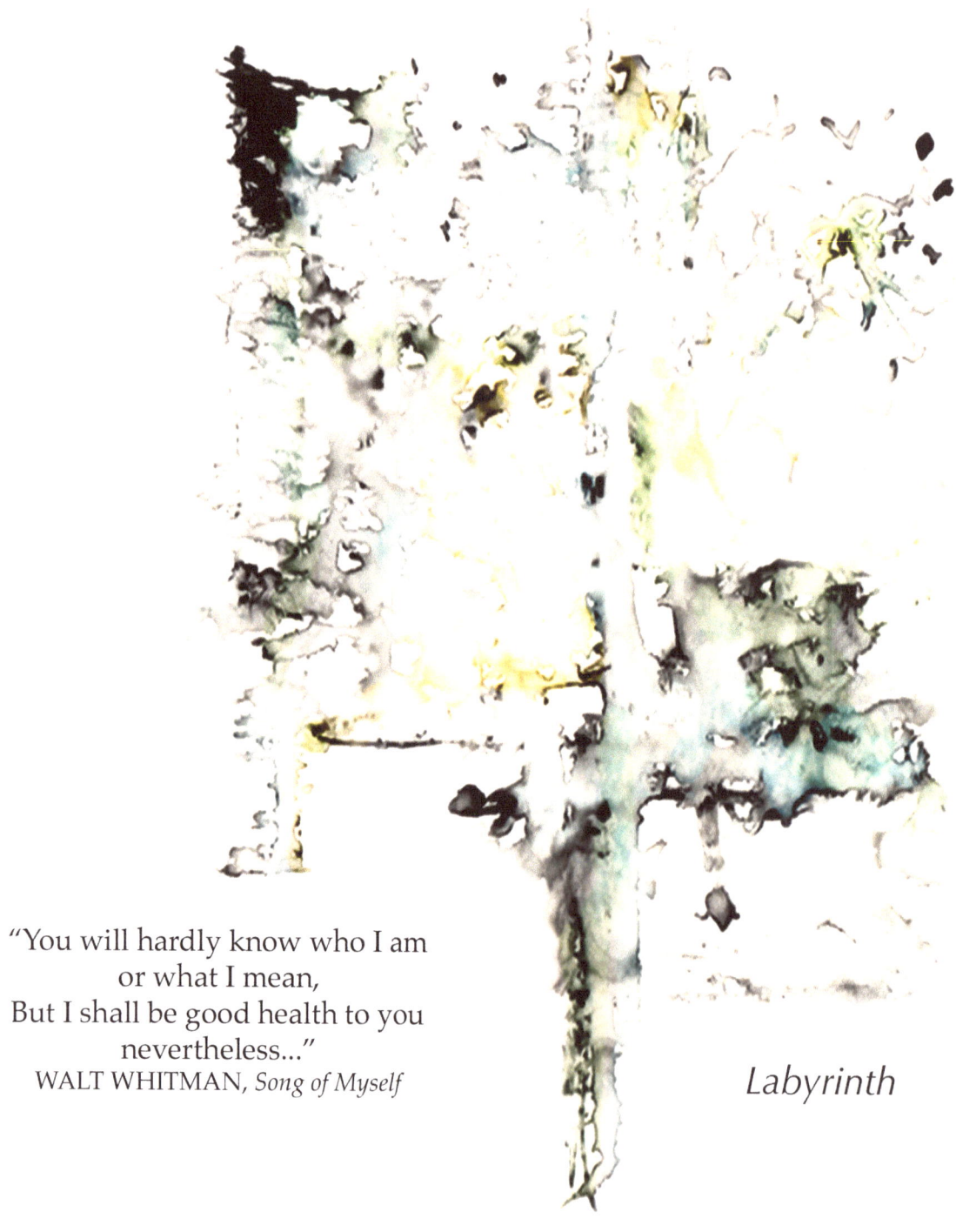

"You will hardly know who I am
or what I mean,
But I shall be good health to you
nevertheless..."
WALT WHITMAN, *Song of Myself*

Labyrinth

Thought Forms

"Ego is no more than identification with form,
which primarily means thought forms."
~ECKHART TOLLE, *A New Earth*, 2005

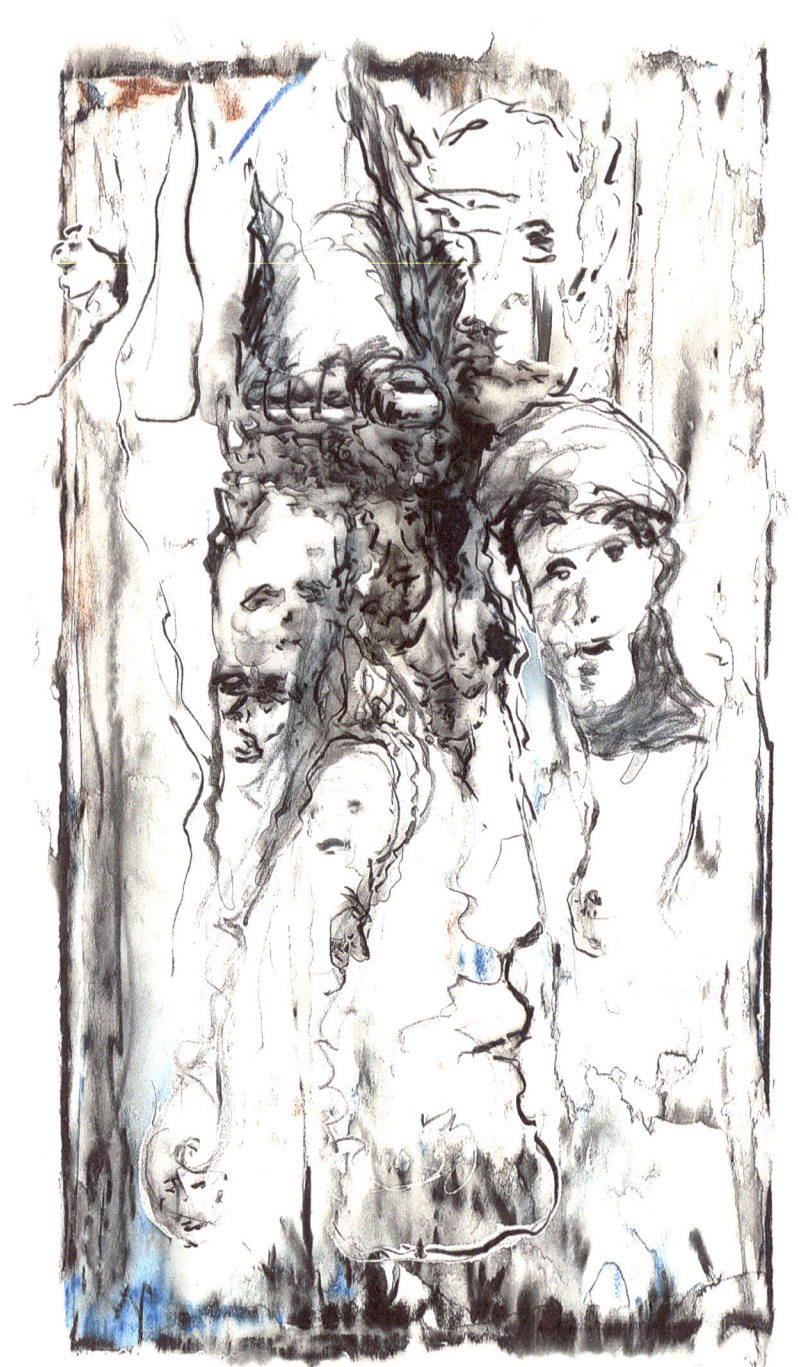

InGathering

Right:
The Gathering 1

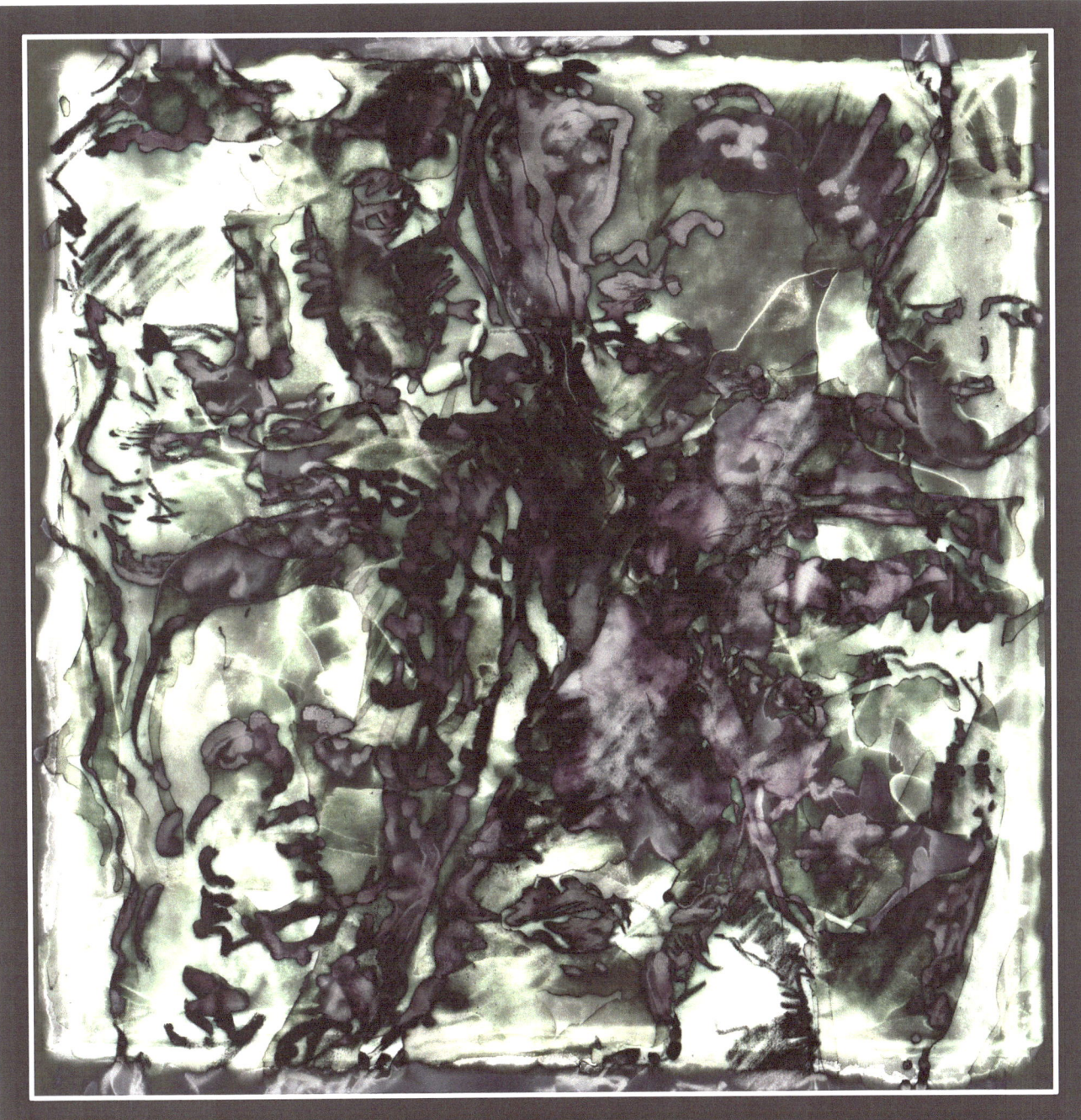

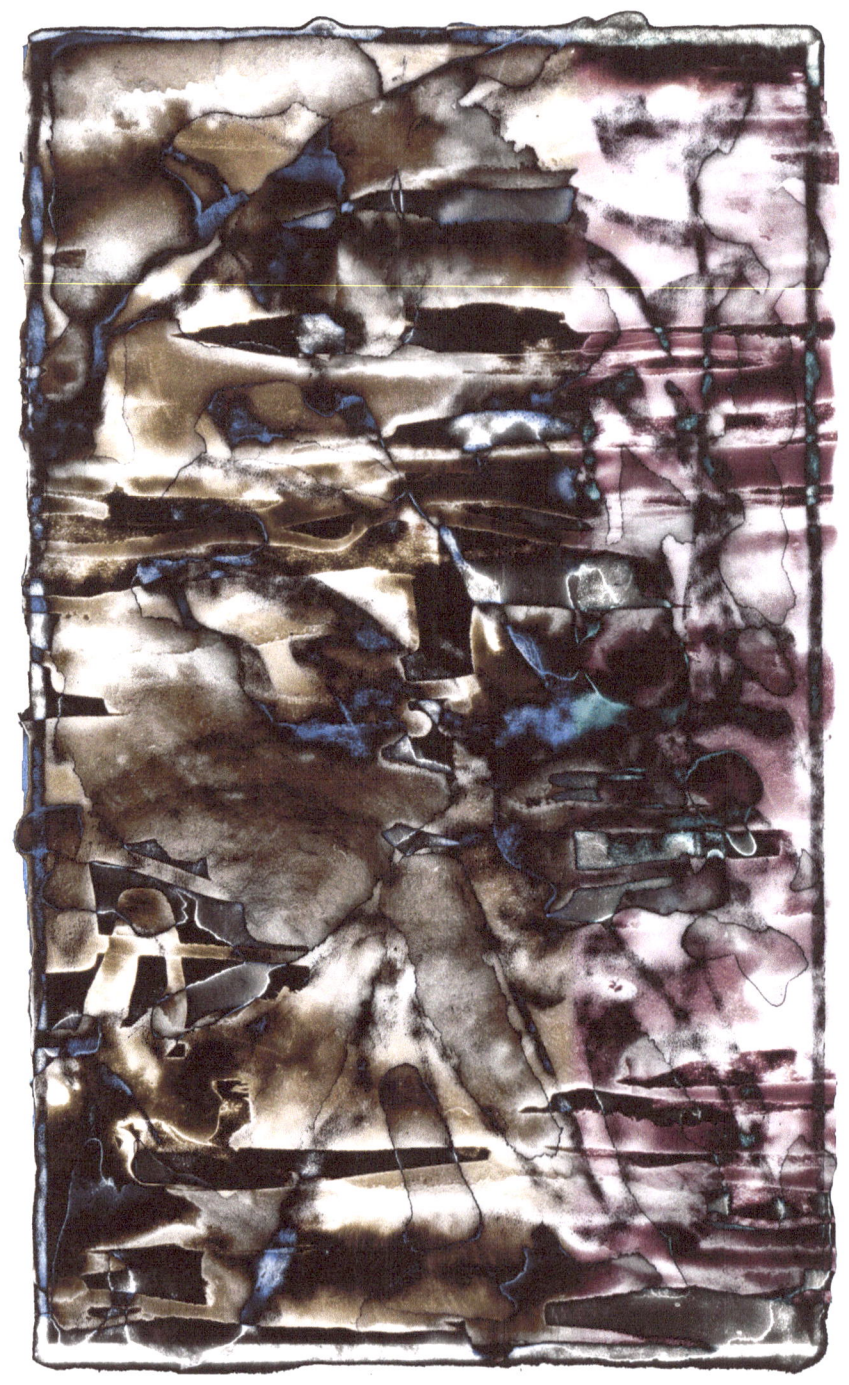

Chaos

"Everywhere I go, I
find the poet has been
there before me."
~CARL JUNG

Adolescence
Transcendence

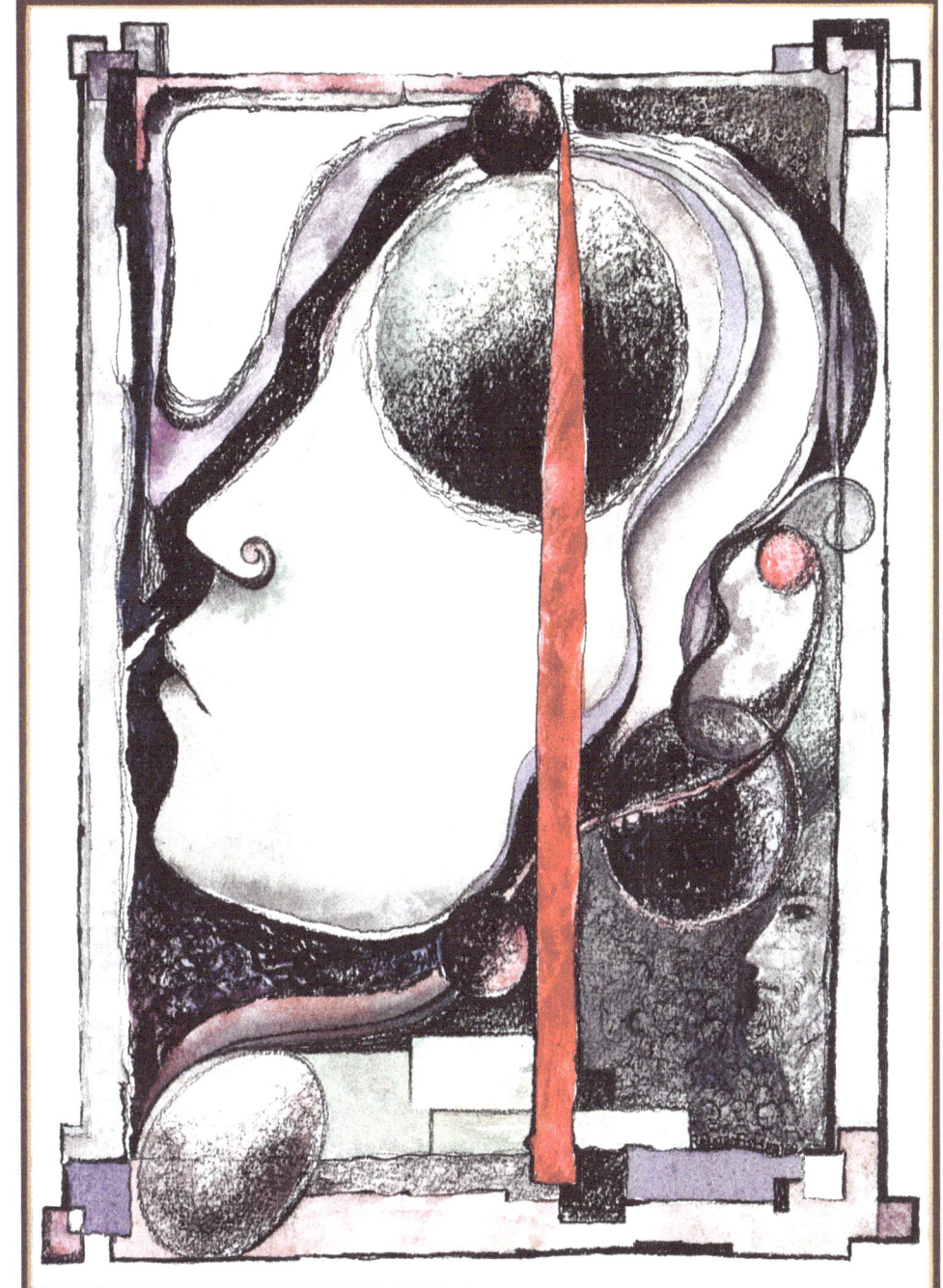

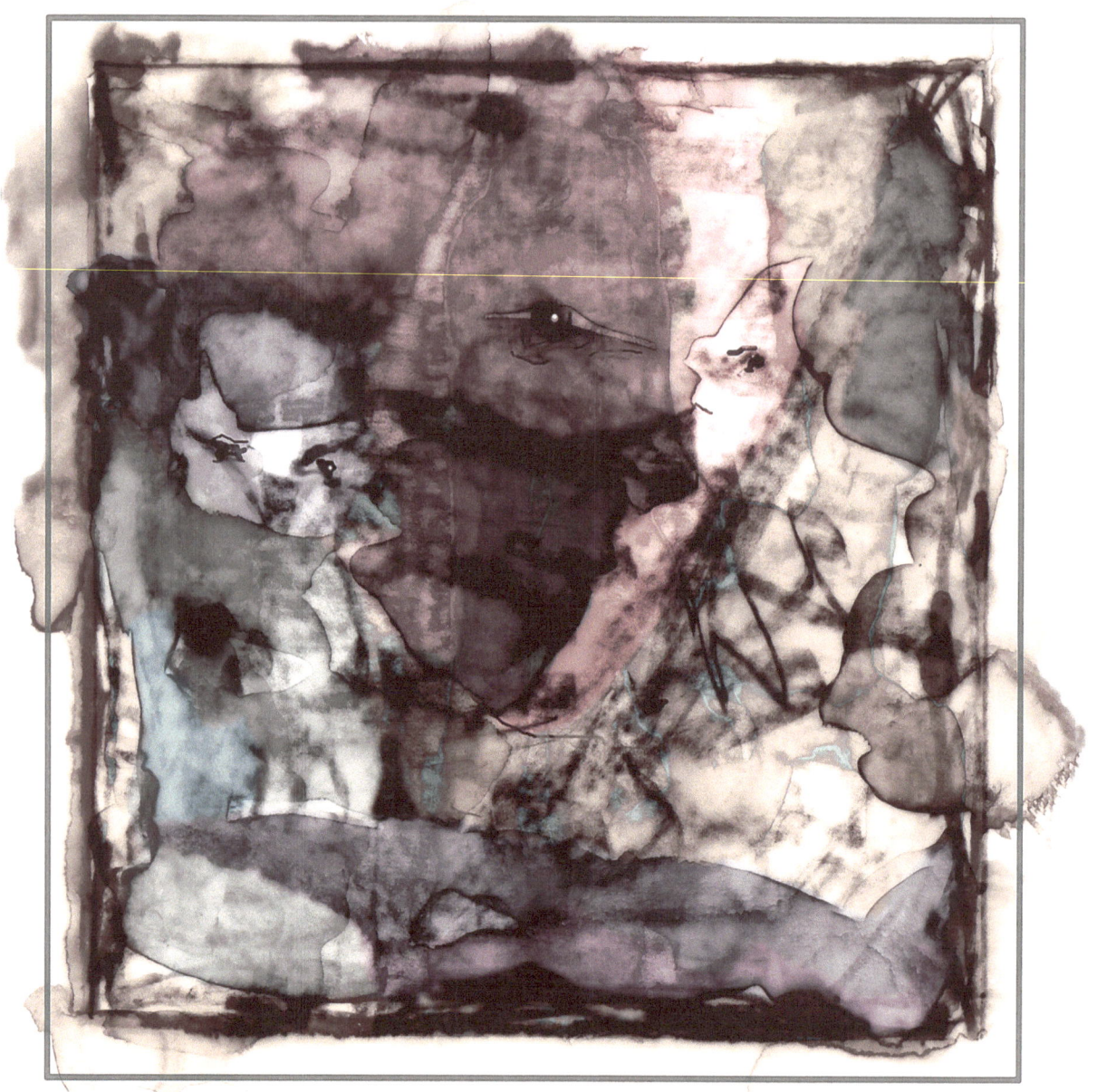

Artists' Focus

"Behind the facade of image and distraction, each person
is an artist...each one of us is doomed and privileged to be
an inner artist who carries and shapes a unique world."
~JOHN O'DONOHUE, *Anam Cara, a Book of Celtic* Wisdom,1997

Compartments

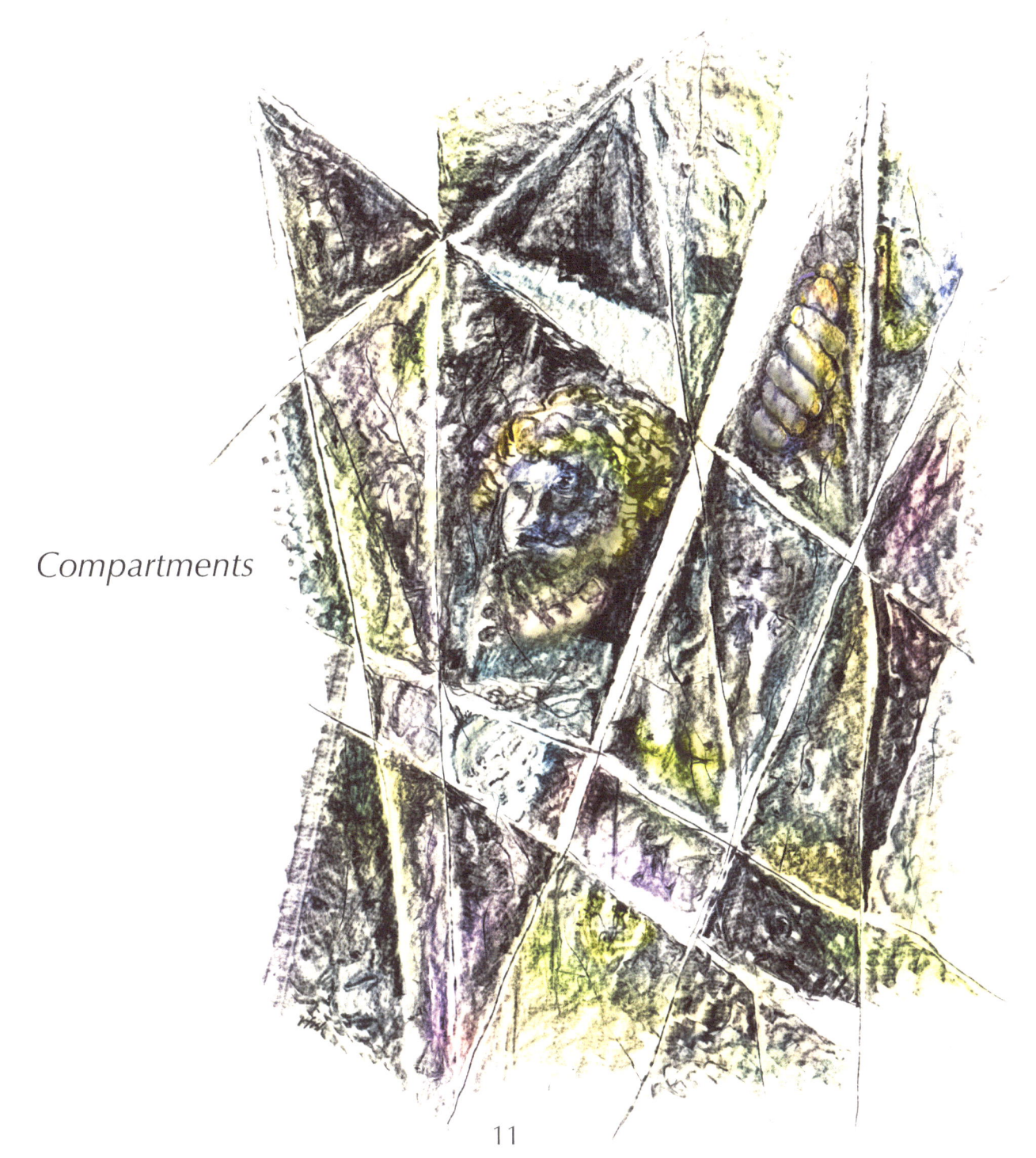

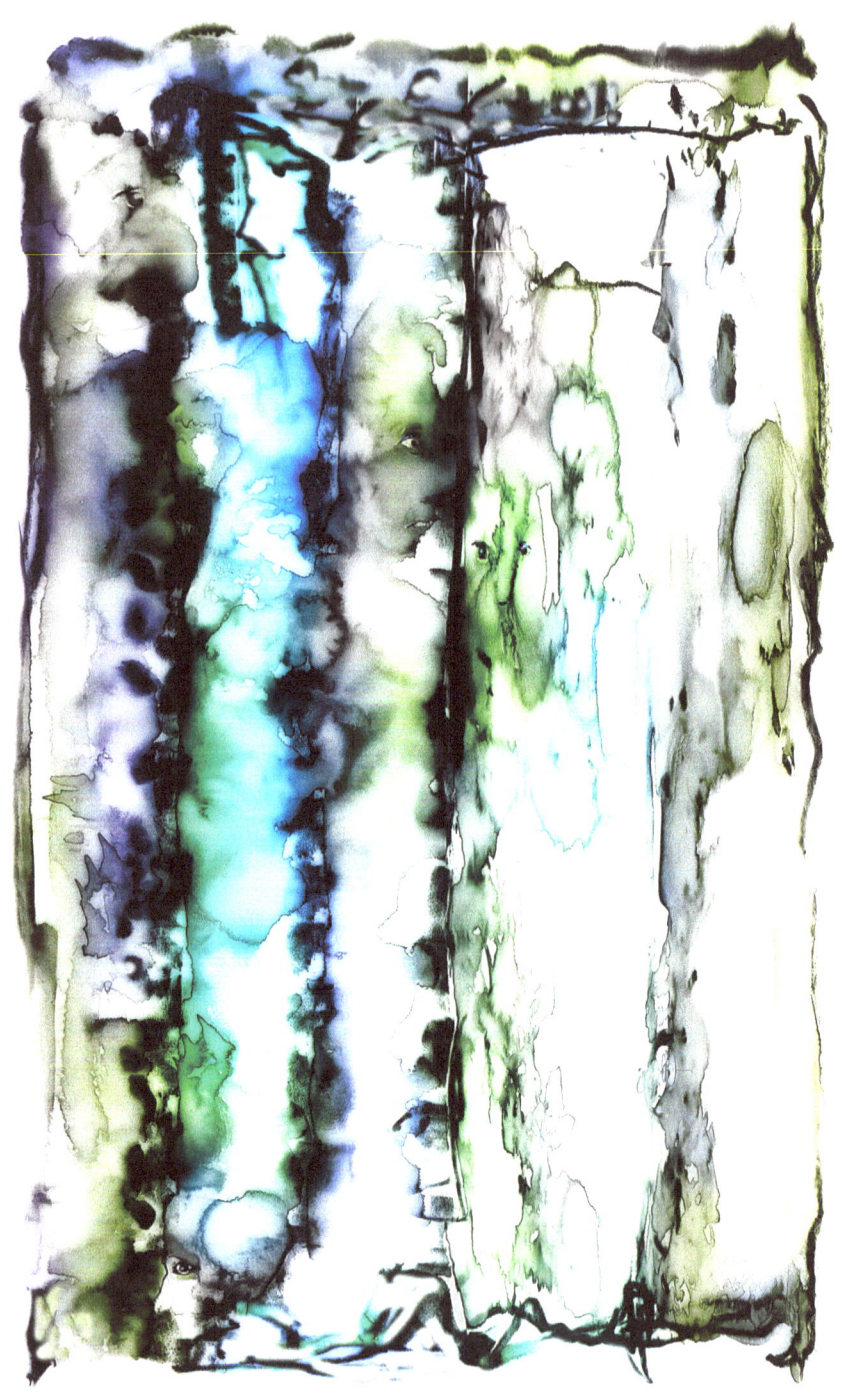

Clones on Hold

"We transform
these things; they
are not real, they
are only the
reflection upon
the polished
surface of our
being ."
~RILKE

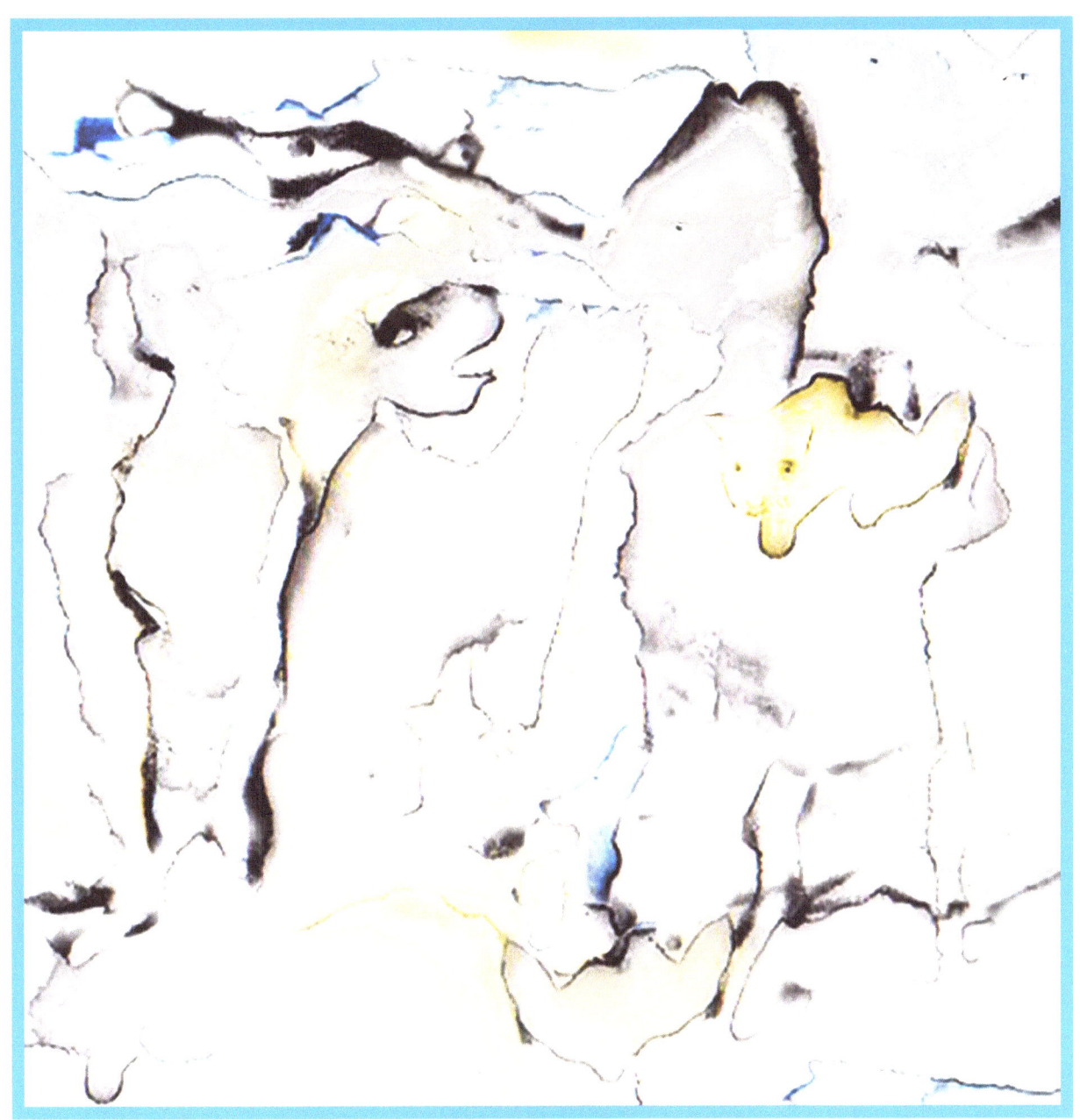

Cat Friends

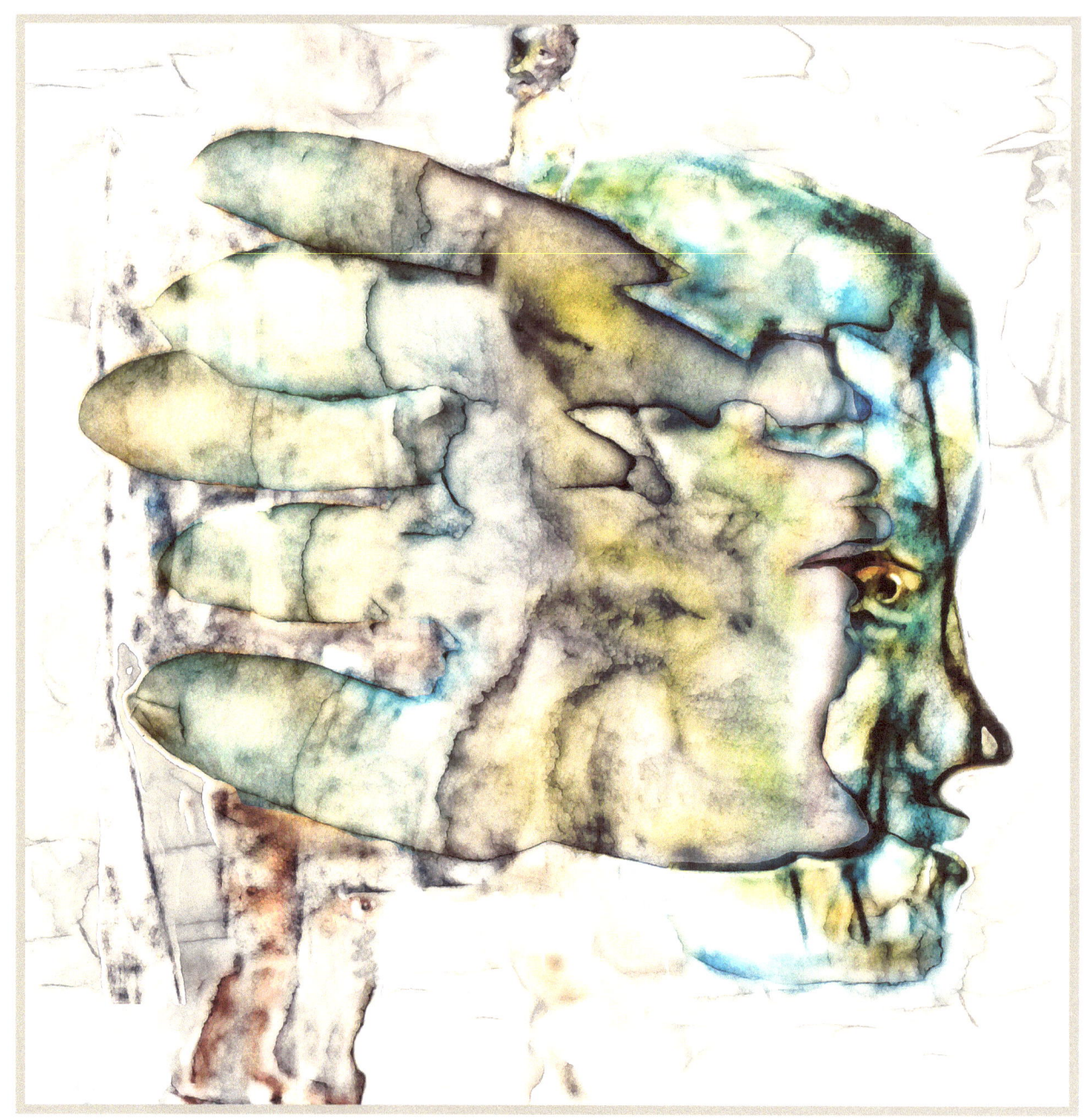

Hand Out

Desire Externalized

"There is no light
without shadow and
no psychic whole-
ness without imper-
fection."
- C.G.JUNG

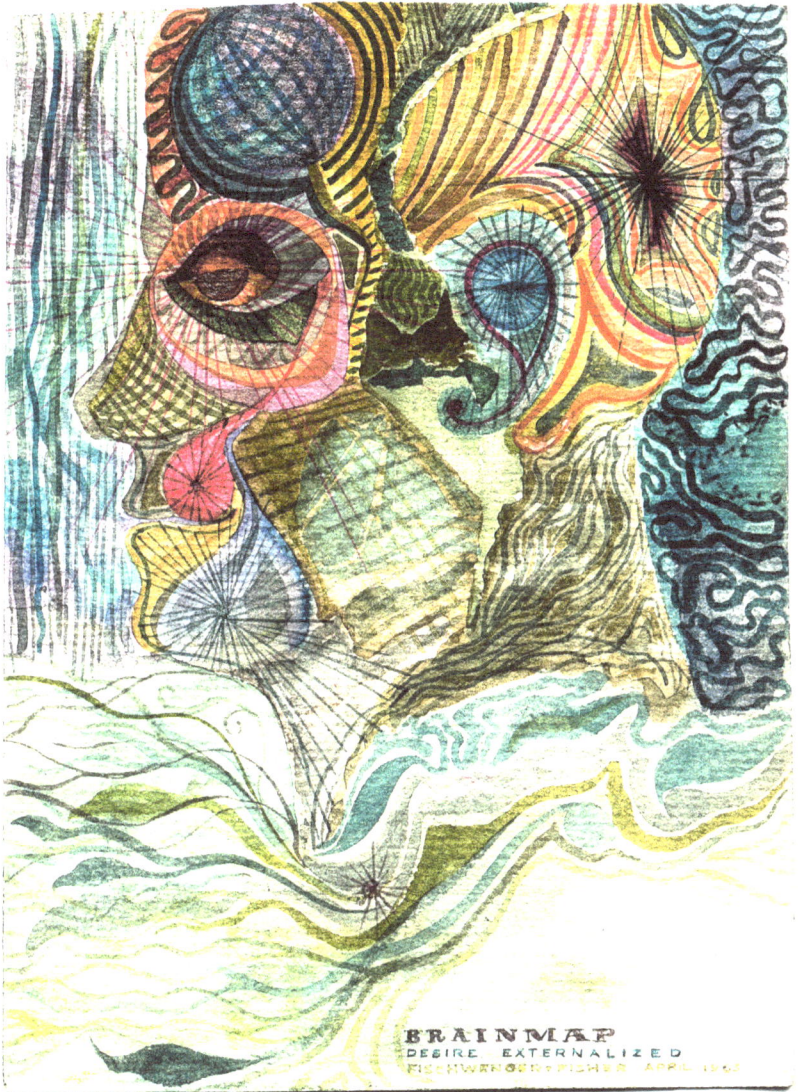

15

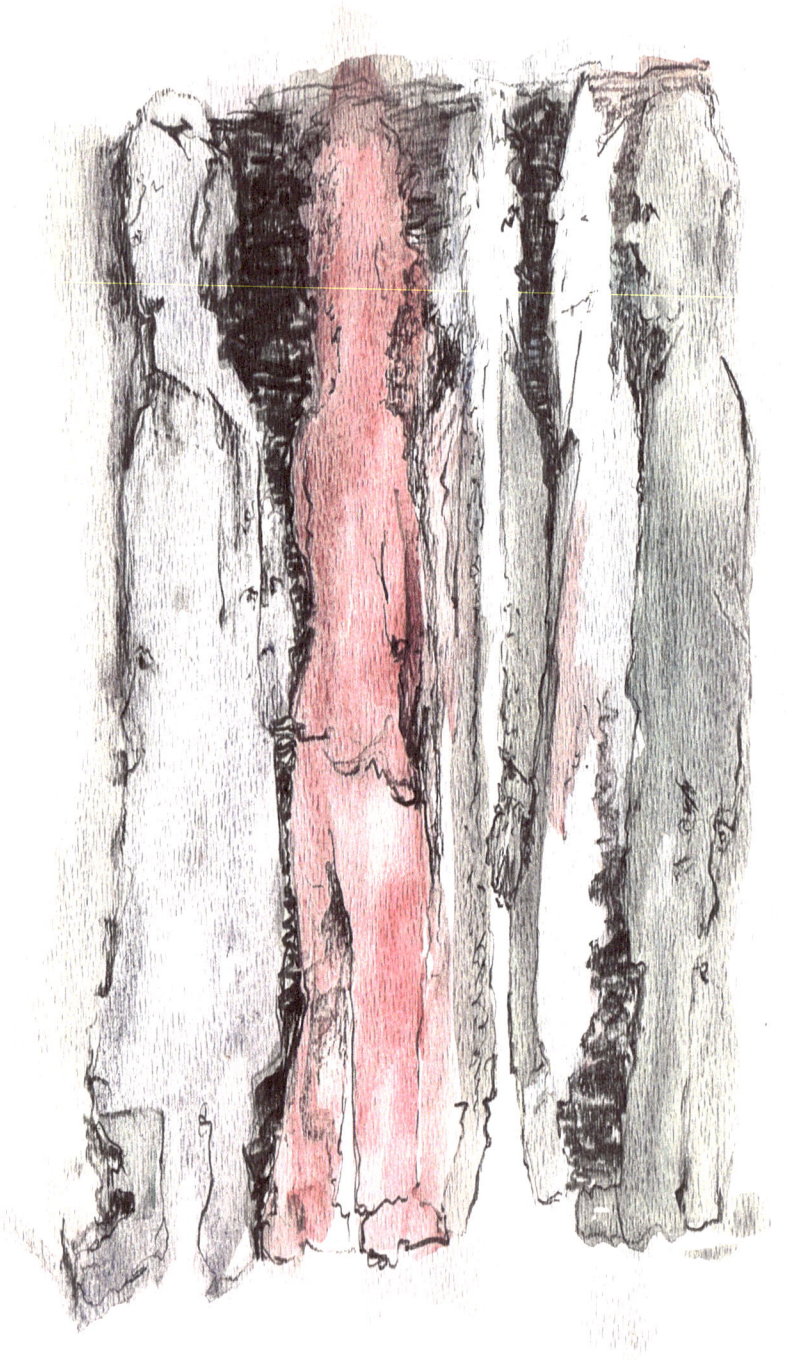

*Which Way
Giacometti?*

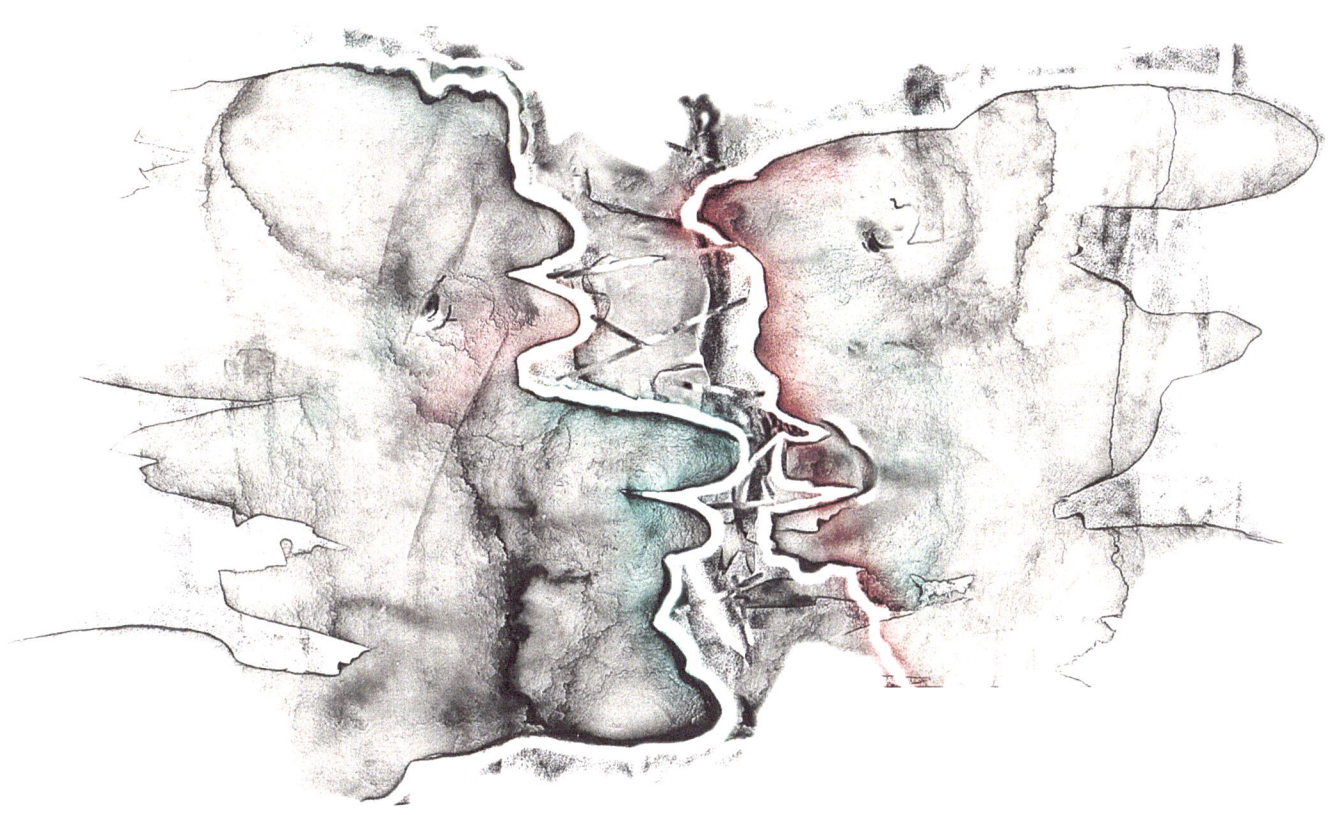

Contentious

"The egoic sense of self needs conflict because its sense of a separate identitiy gets strengthened in fighting against this or that, and in demonstrating that this is "me" and that is not "me".
~ECKHART TOLLE, *Stillness Speaks* 2003

17

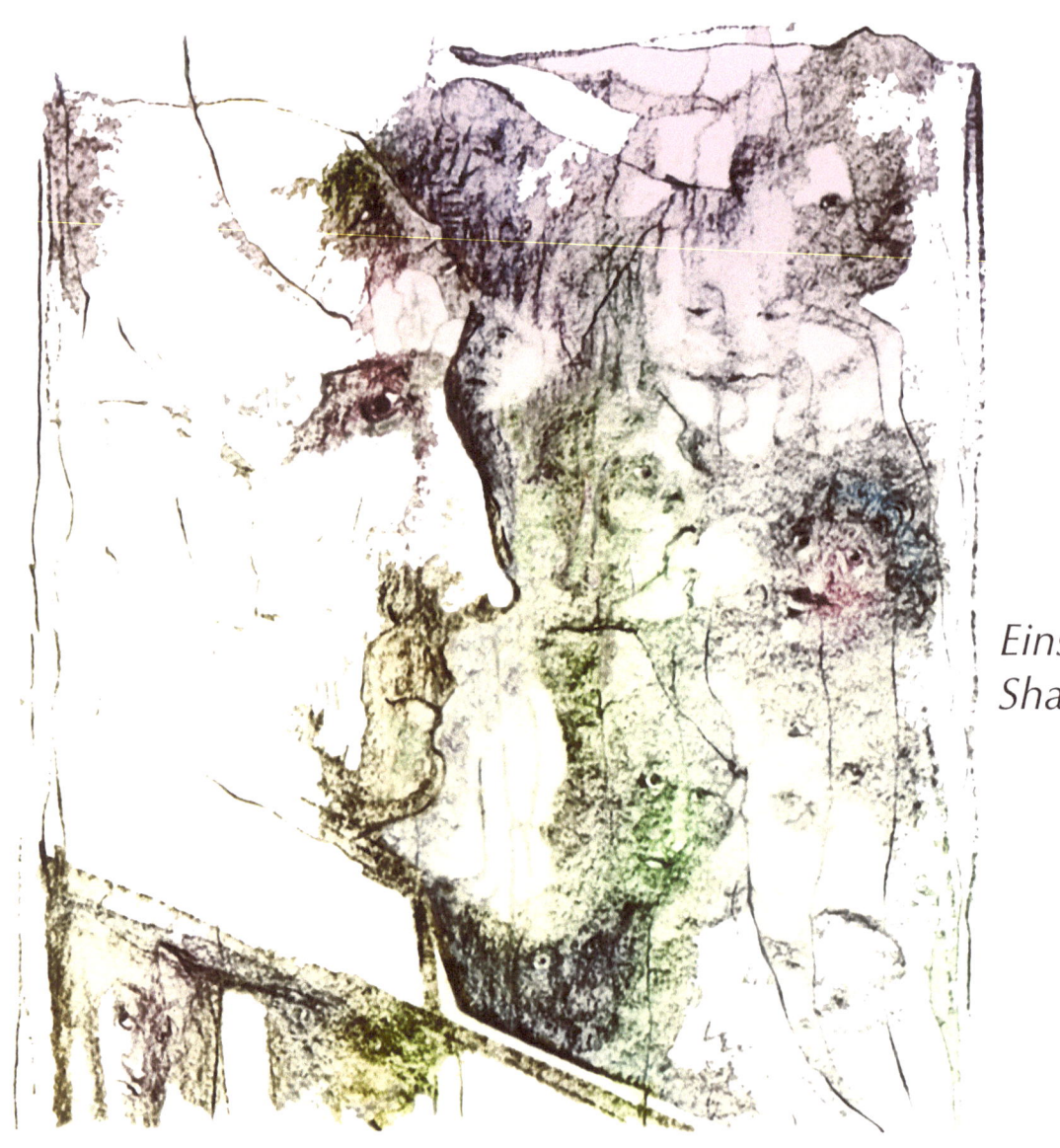

Einstein
Shaving

"Imagination is more important than knowledge."~EINSTEIN

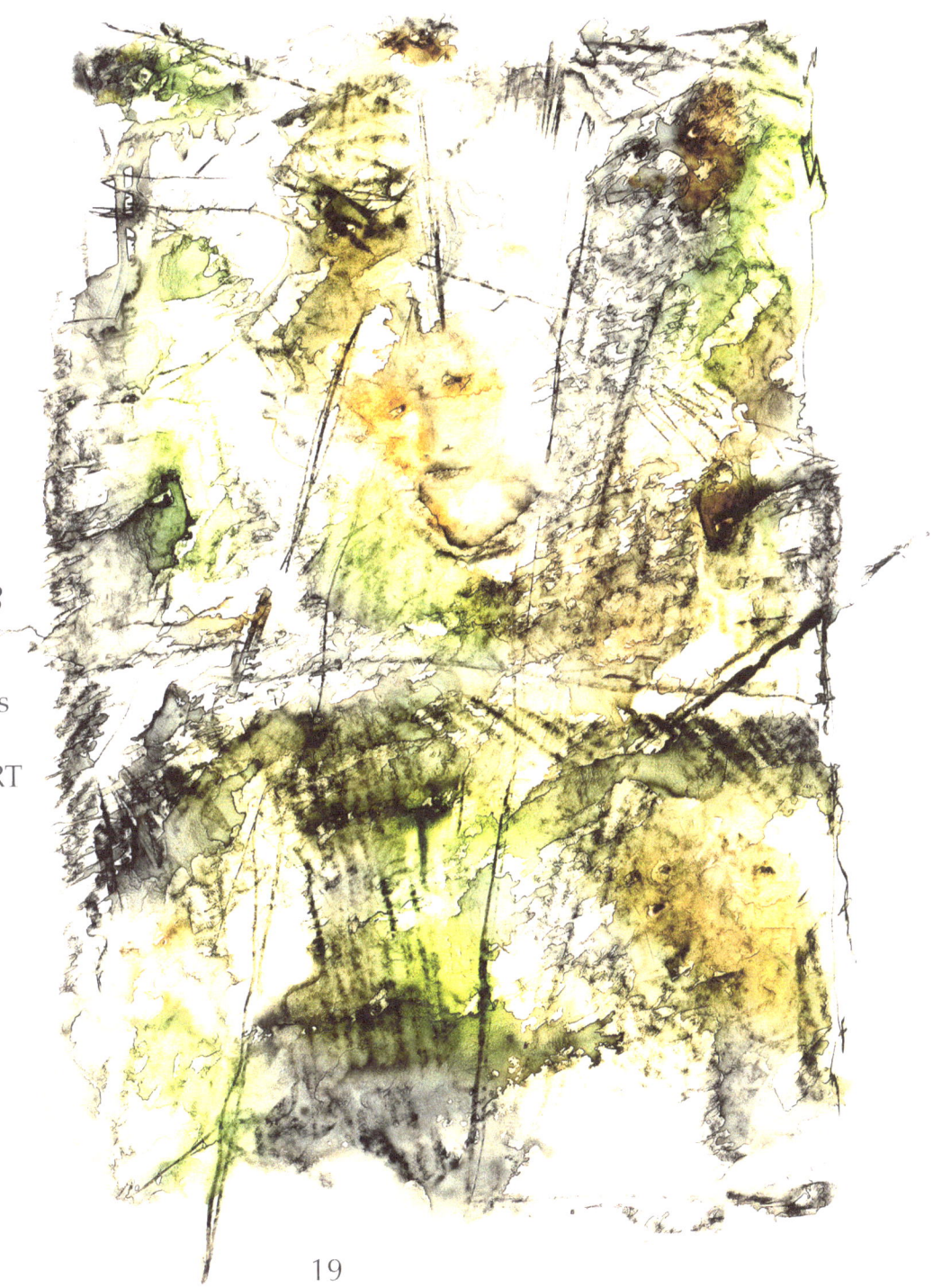

Ego Chatter 3

A variation of this
image is seen in
MINDWORKS ART
Volume 1

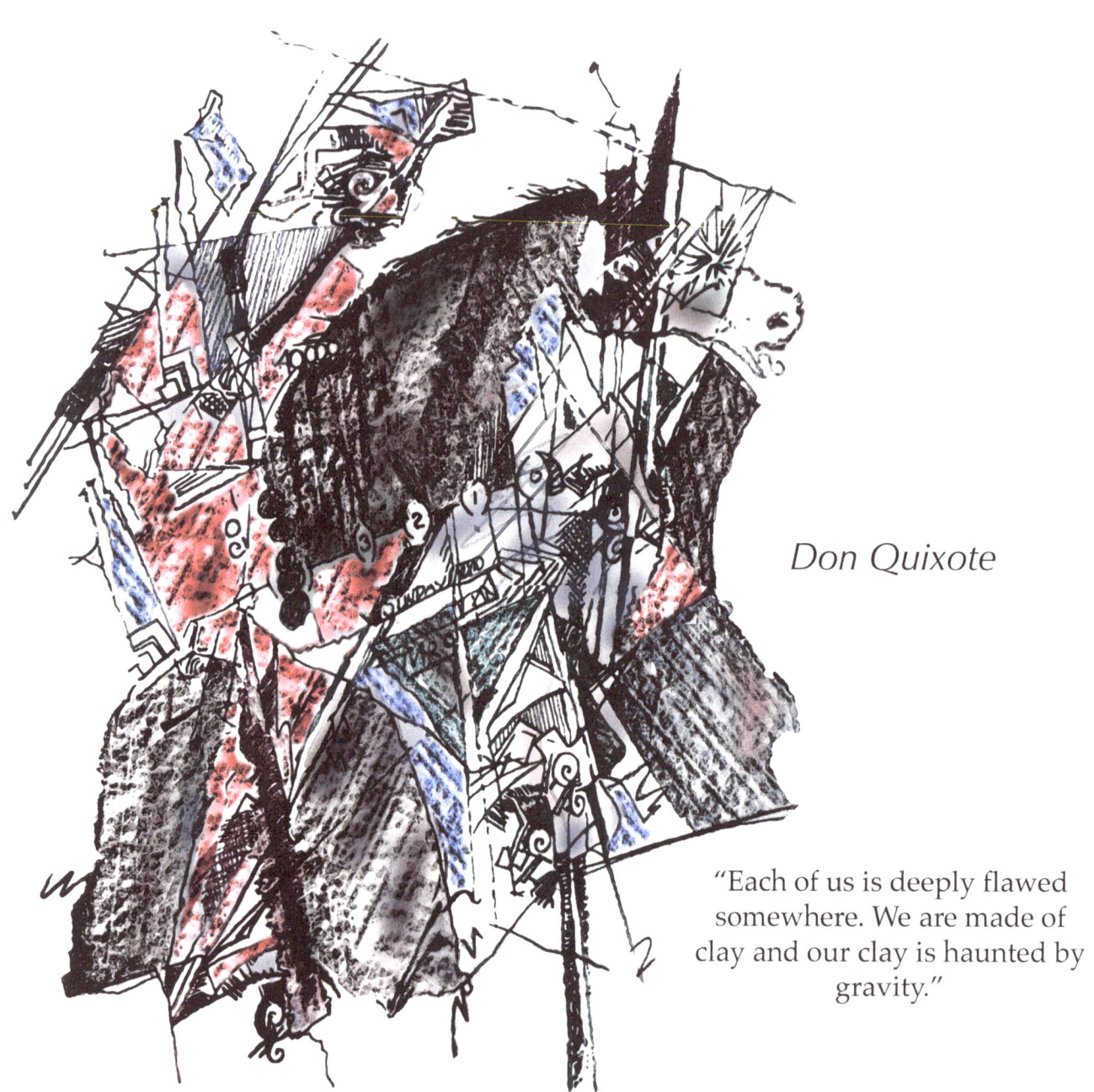

Don Quixote

"Each of us is deeply flawed somewhere. We are made of clay and our clay is haunted by gravity."

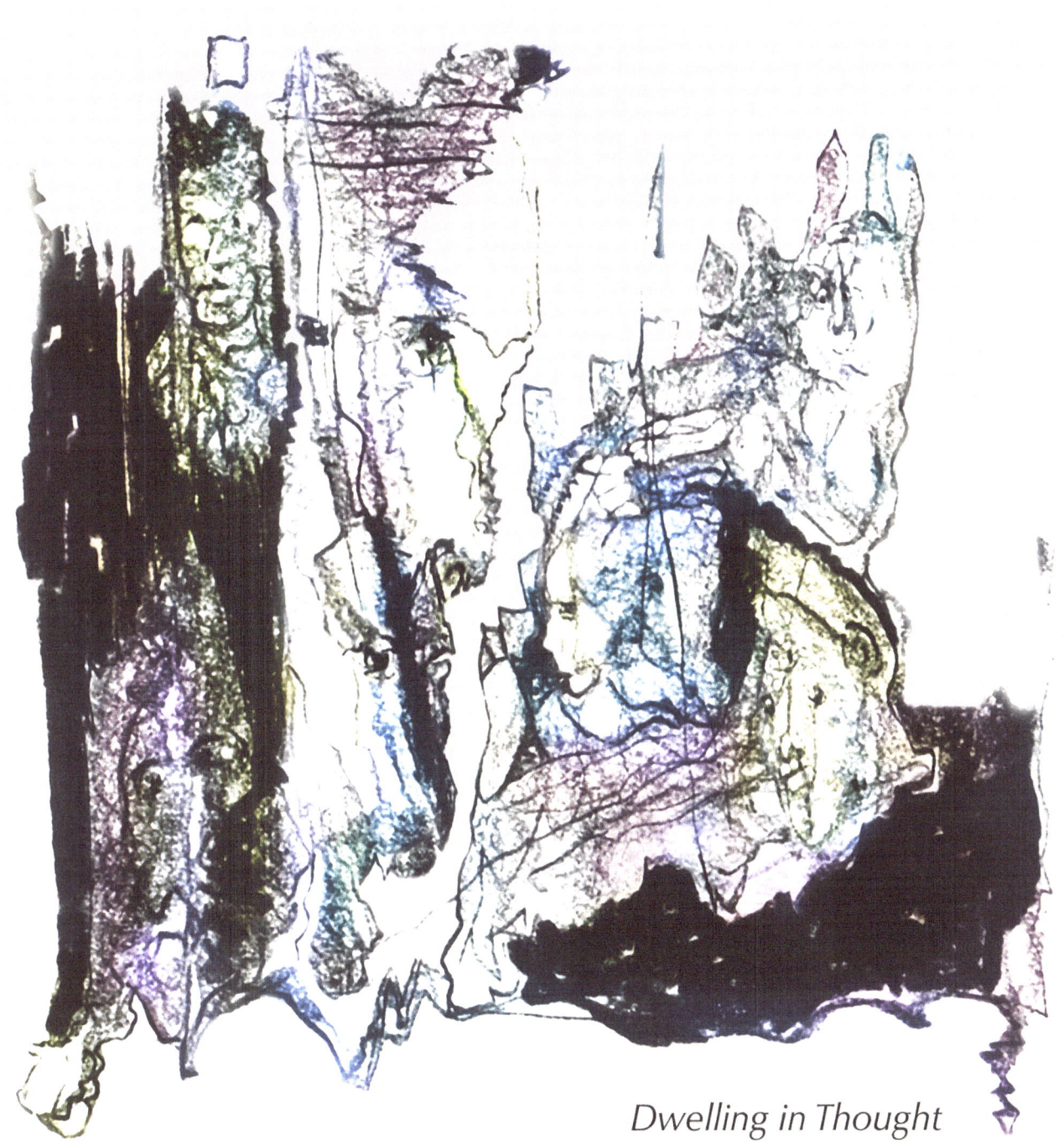

Dwelling in Thought

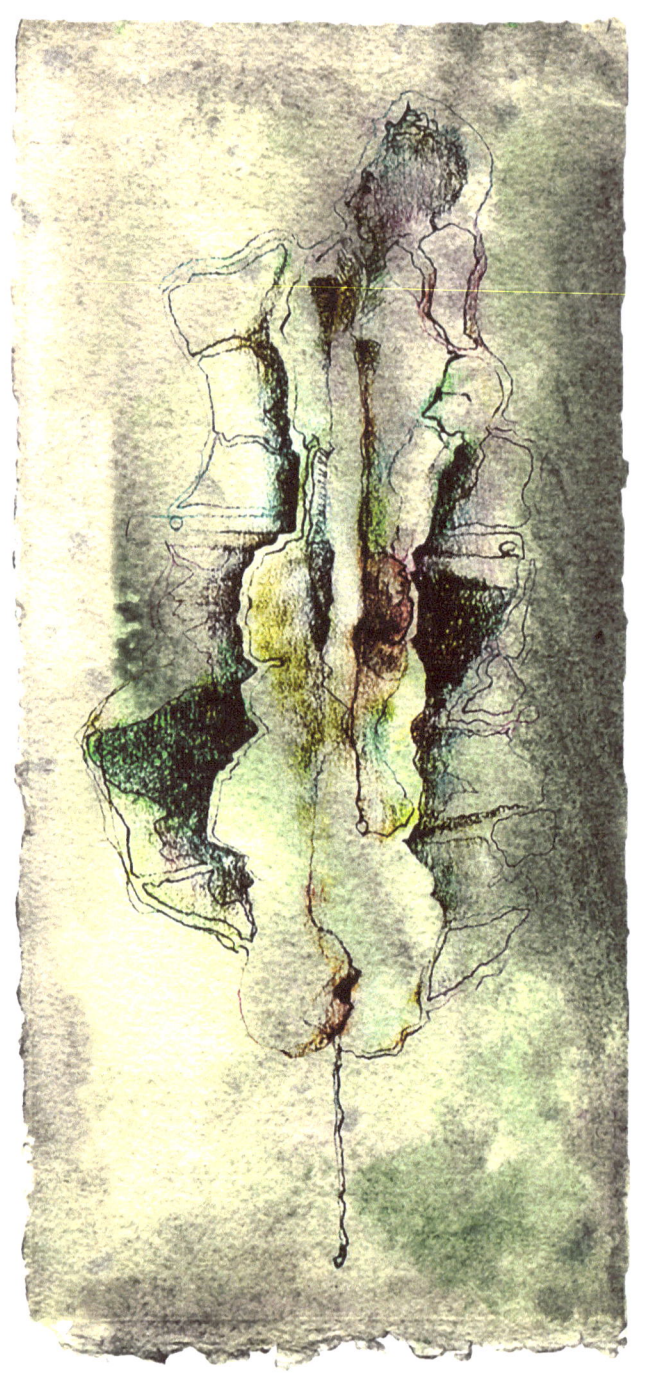

I AM in Green Texture

"I am not my thoughts,
emotions, sense perceptions,
and experiences.
I am not the content of
my life.
I am Life.
I am the space in which all
things happen.
I am consciousness.
I am the Now.
I Am."
~ECKHART TOLLE,
Stillness Speaks

The Fabric of Life

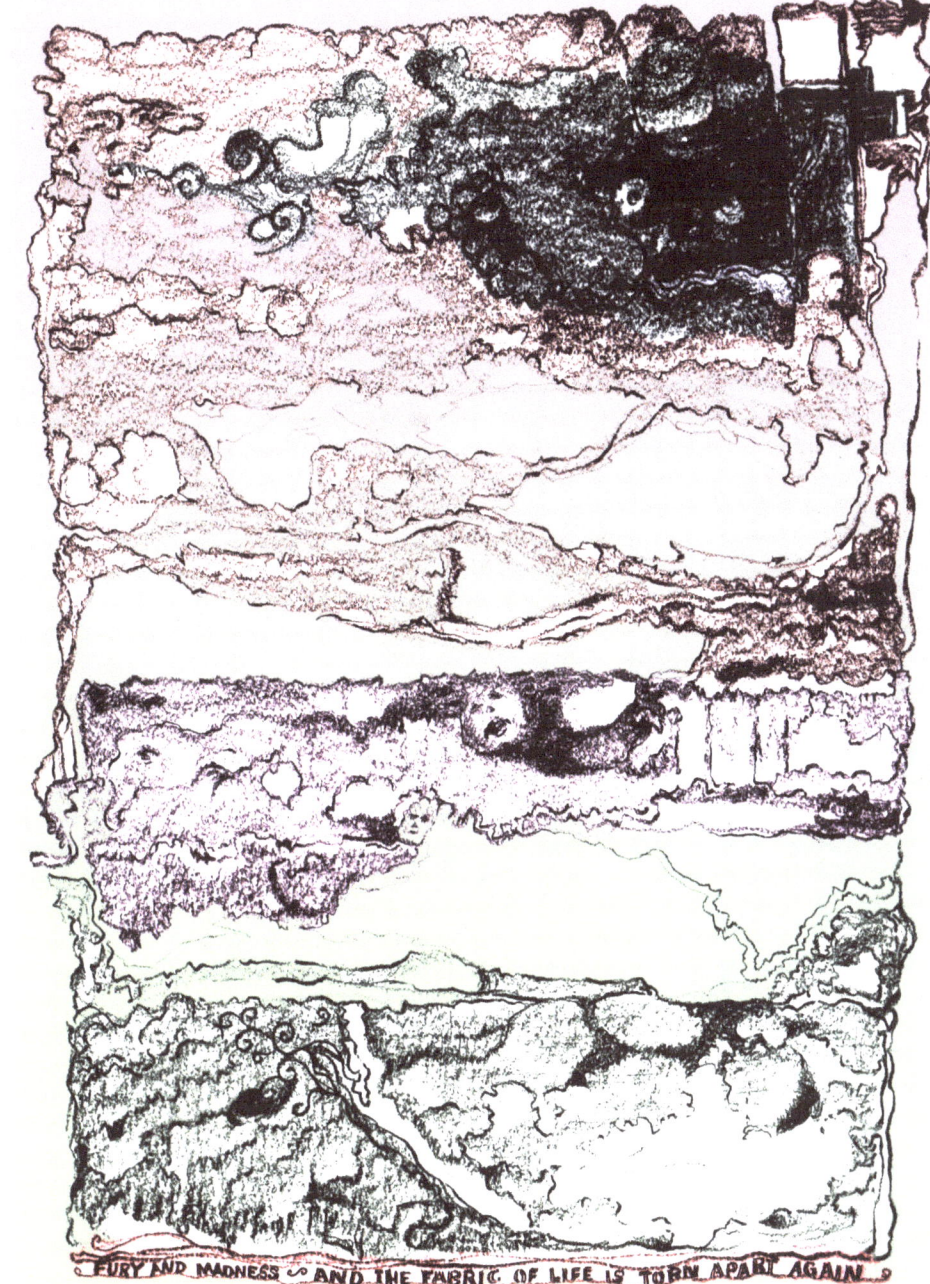

FURY AND MADNESS ~ AND THE FABRIC OF LIFE IS TORN APART AGAIN

23

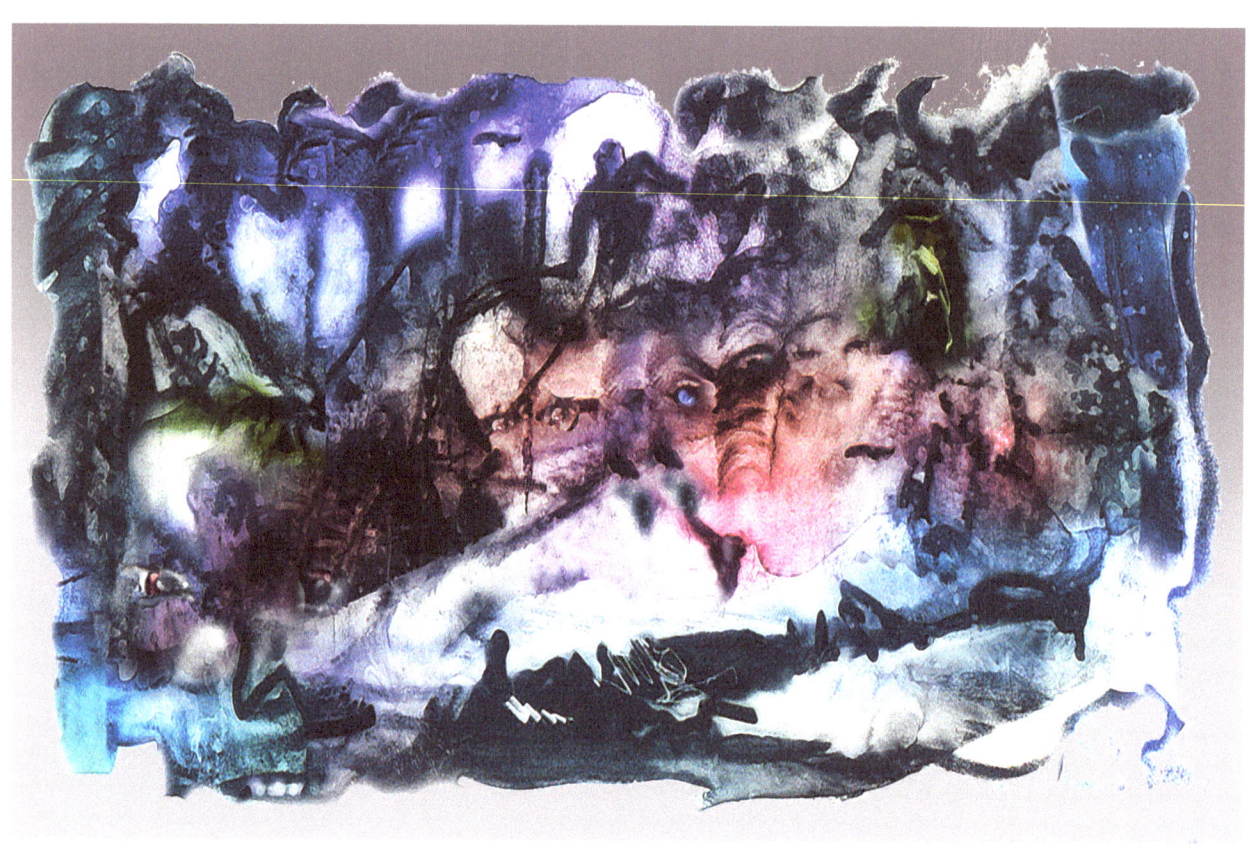

InnerScape 3

"What will be left of all the fear and wanting associated with your prob-
lematic life situations that every day takes up most of your attention? A
dash--one or two inches long, between the date of birth and date of death
on your gravestone. To the egoic self, this is a depressing thought.
To you, it is liberating."

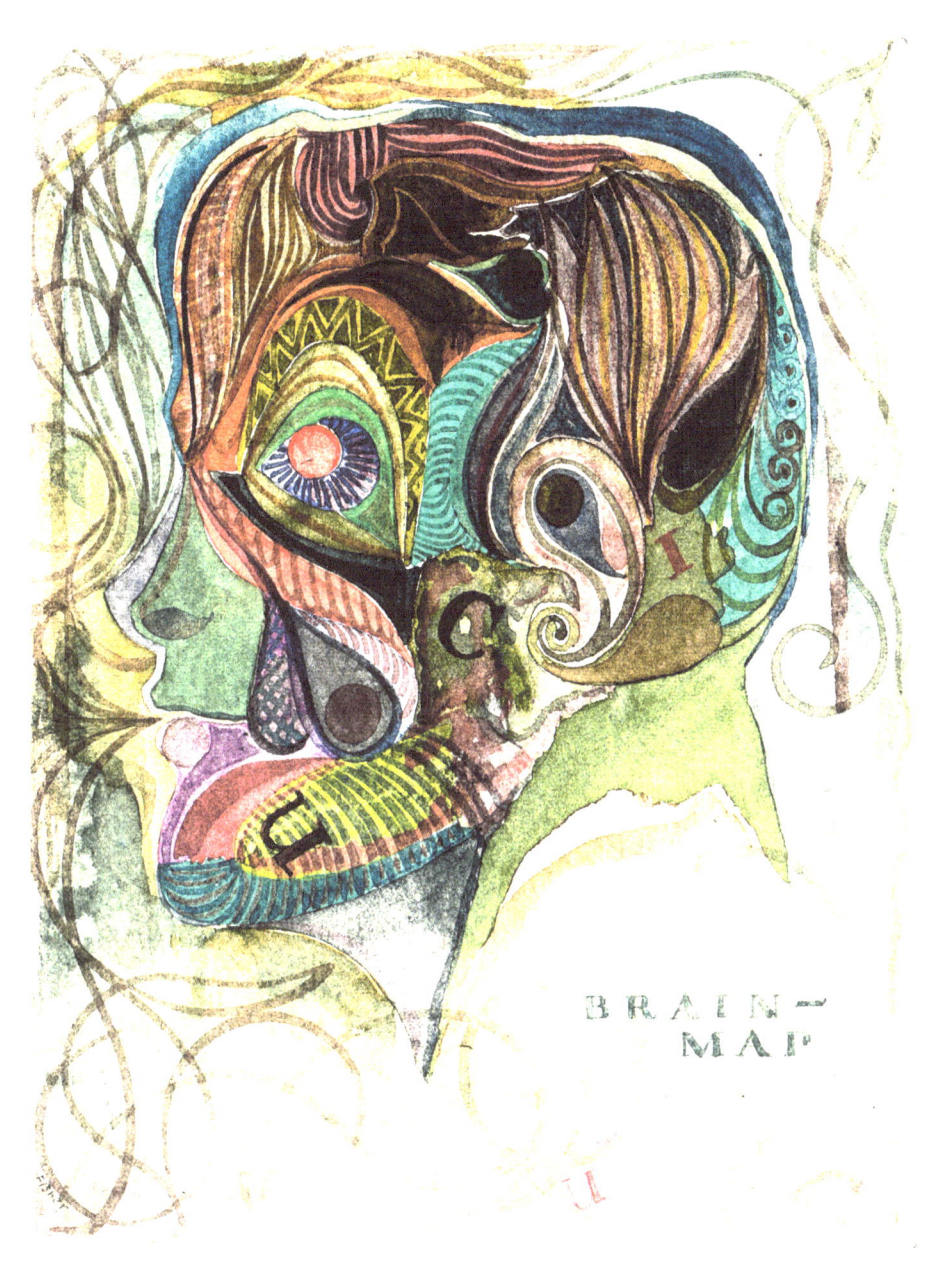

I See You

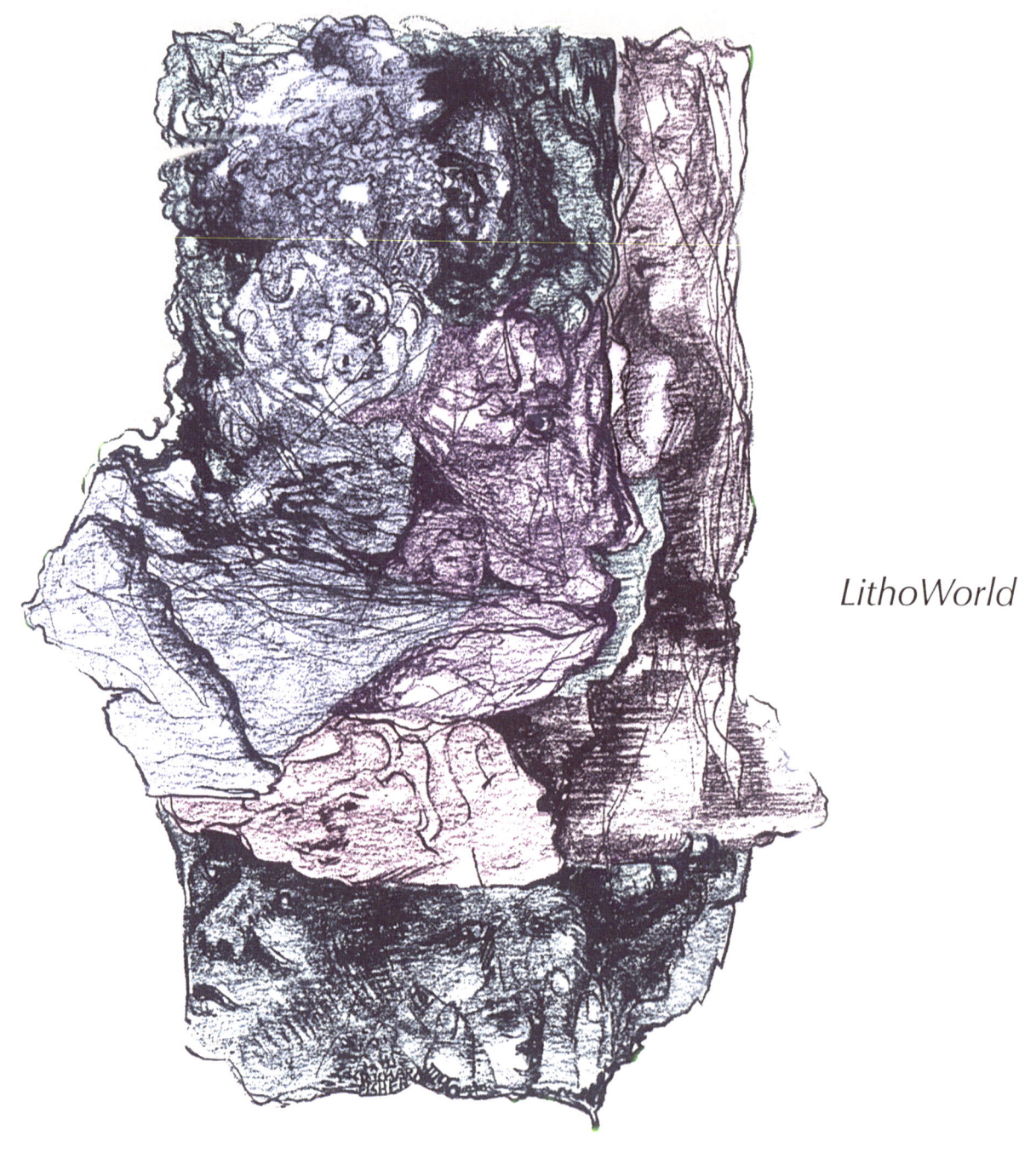

LithoWorld

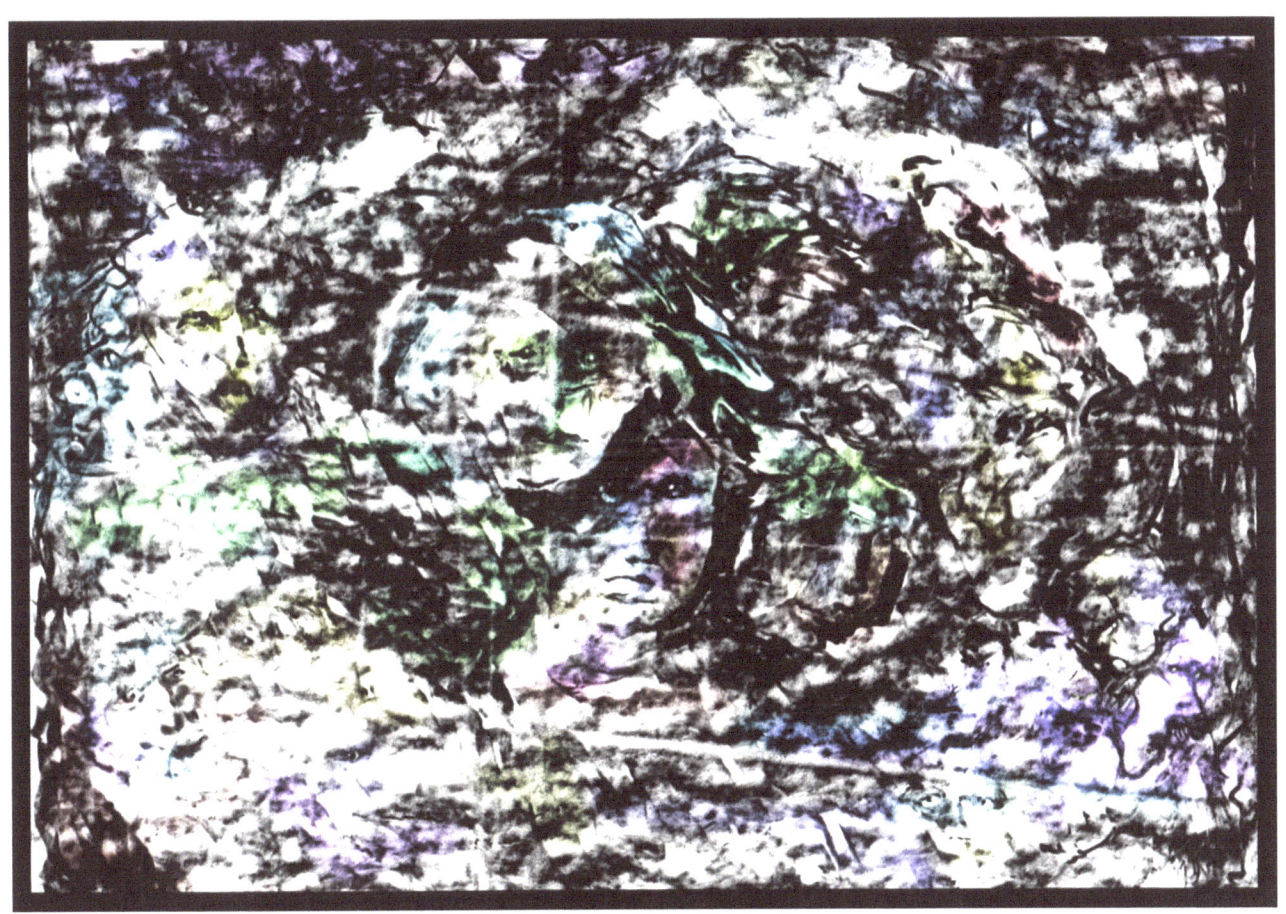

The Madness of This World

"The grasp becomes tighter around the people, people from all walks of life.
No one is immune. The desperate man in the middle is moments from being
devoured while others still struggle.
The bird feels no pressure from the grip. Perhaps it is free of man's pressures.
The grasp is certainly a horrible trap existing only in man's mind.
I hope that there is a way out. Maybe the bird can show the way."
~Anonymous Commentary

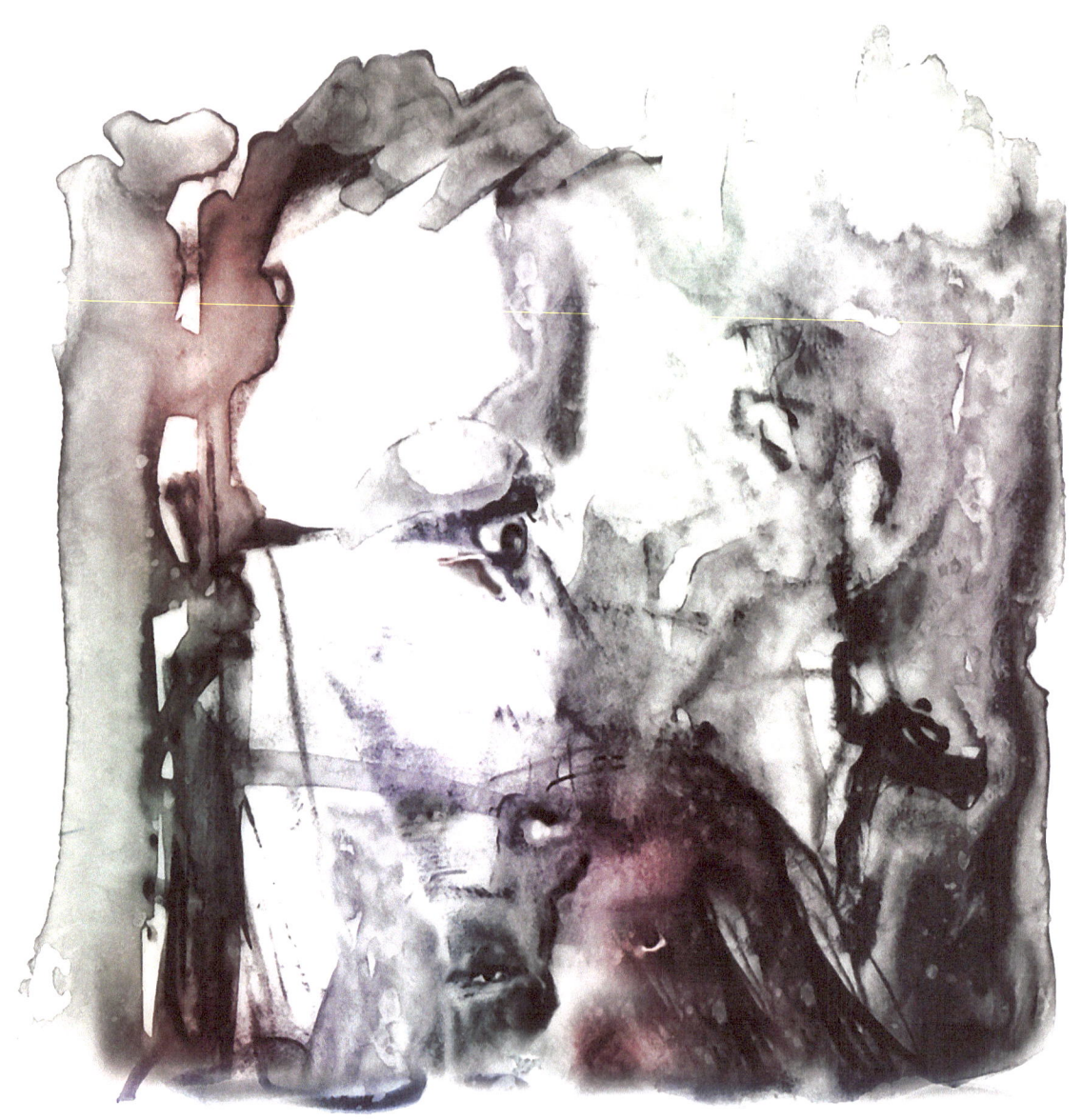

Insanity

"Paradoxicallly, things are getting worse
and better at the same time, although
the worse is more apparent because it
makes so much 'noise.'"
~ECKHART TOLLE, *Stillness Speaks, 2003*

28

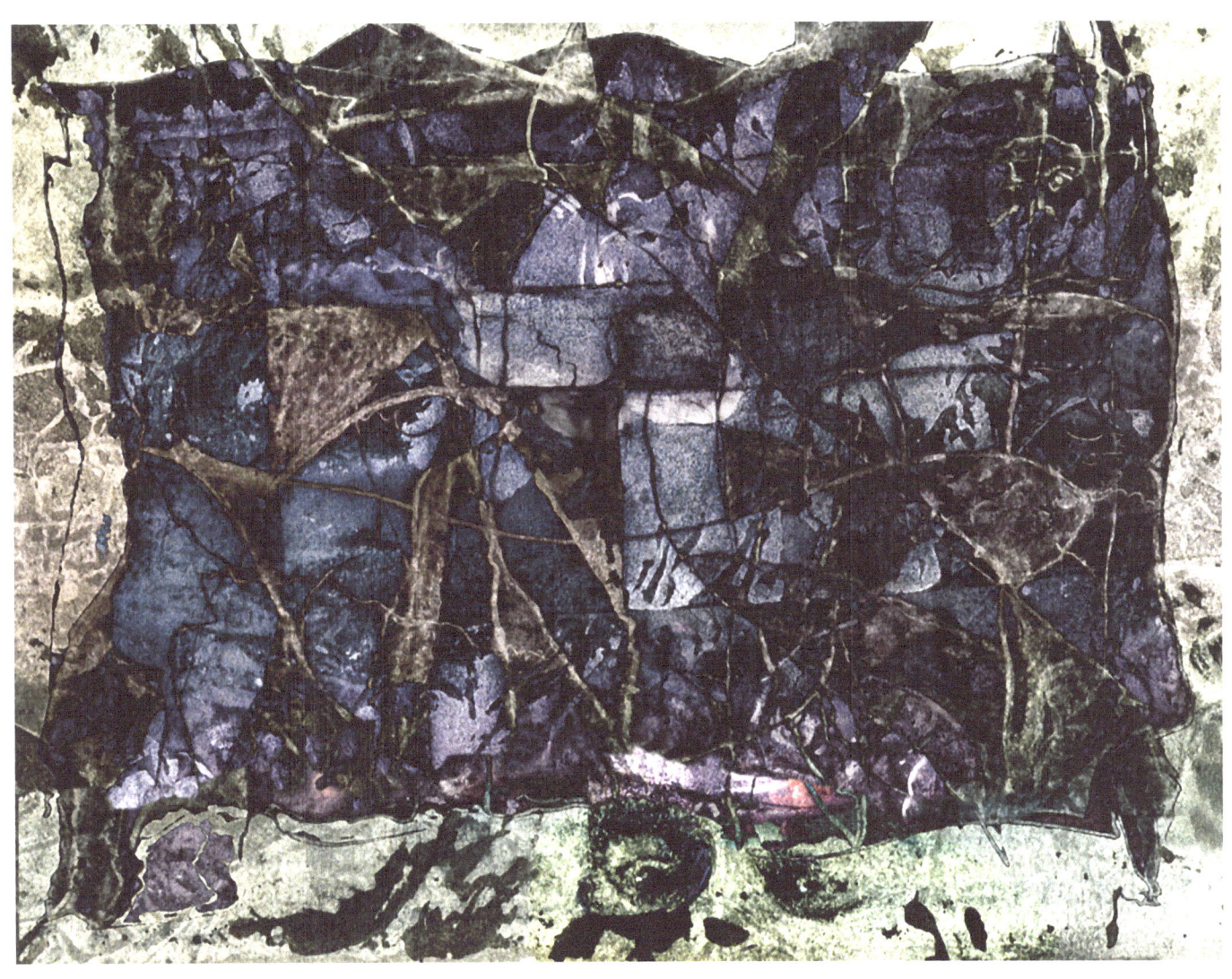

InnerScape 2

"All creativity comes out of inner spaciousness."
~ECKHART TOLLE, *A New Earth*, 2005

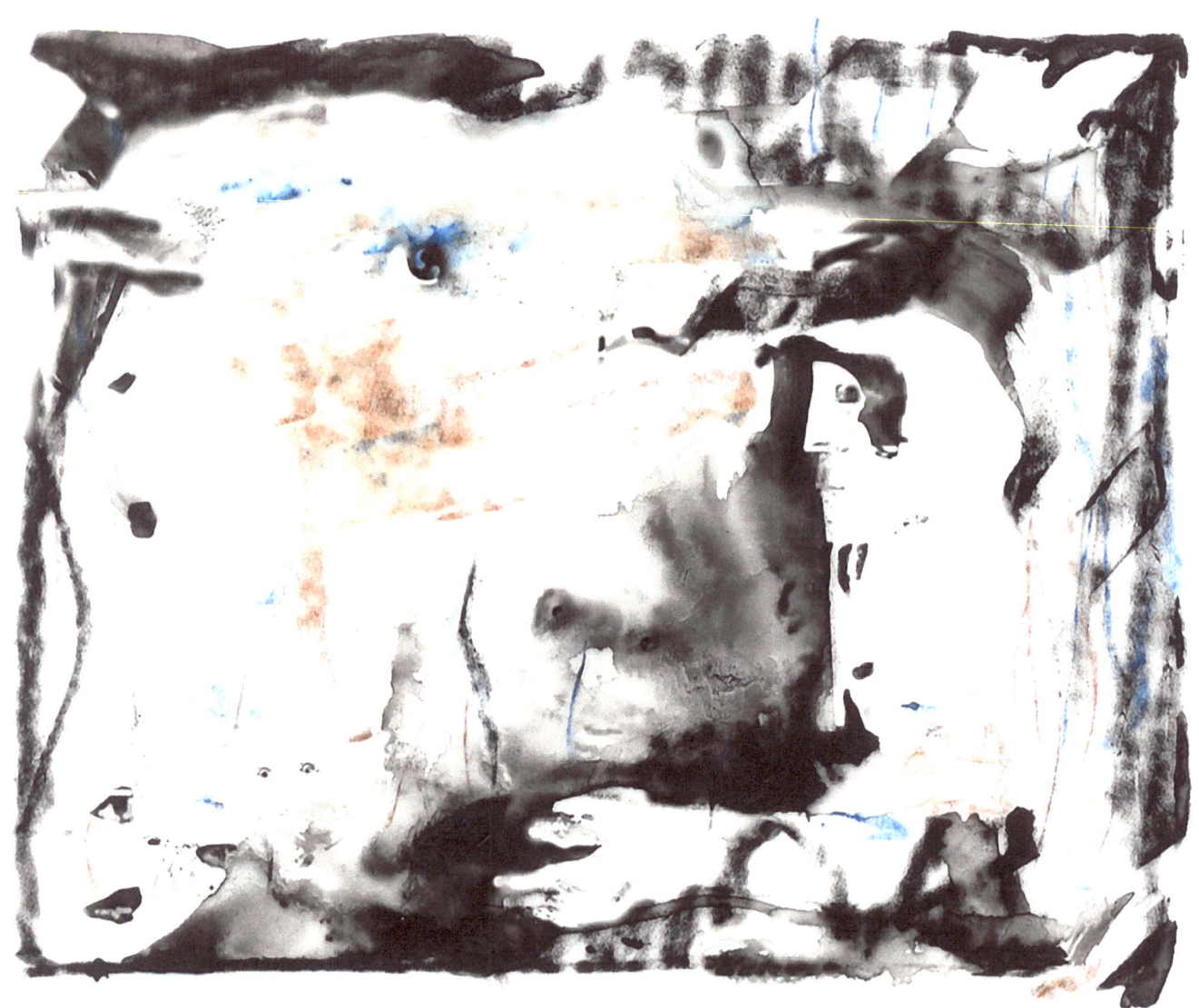

Jockey

"Life will give you whatever experience is most
helpful for the evolution of your consciousness."
~ECKHART TOLLE, A New Earth, 2005

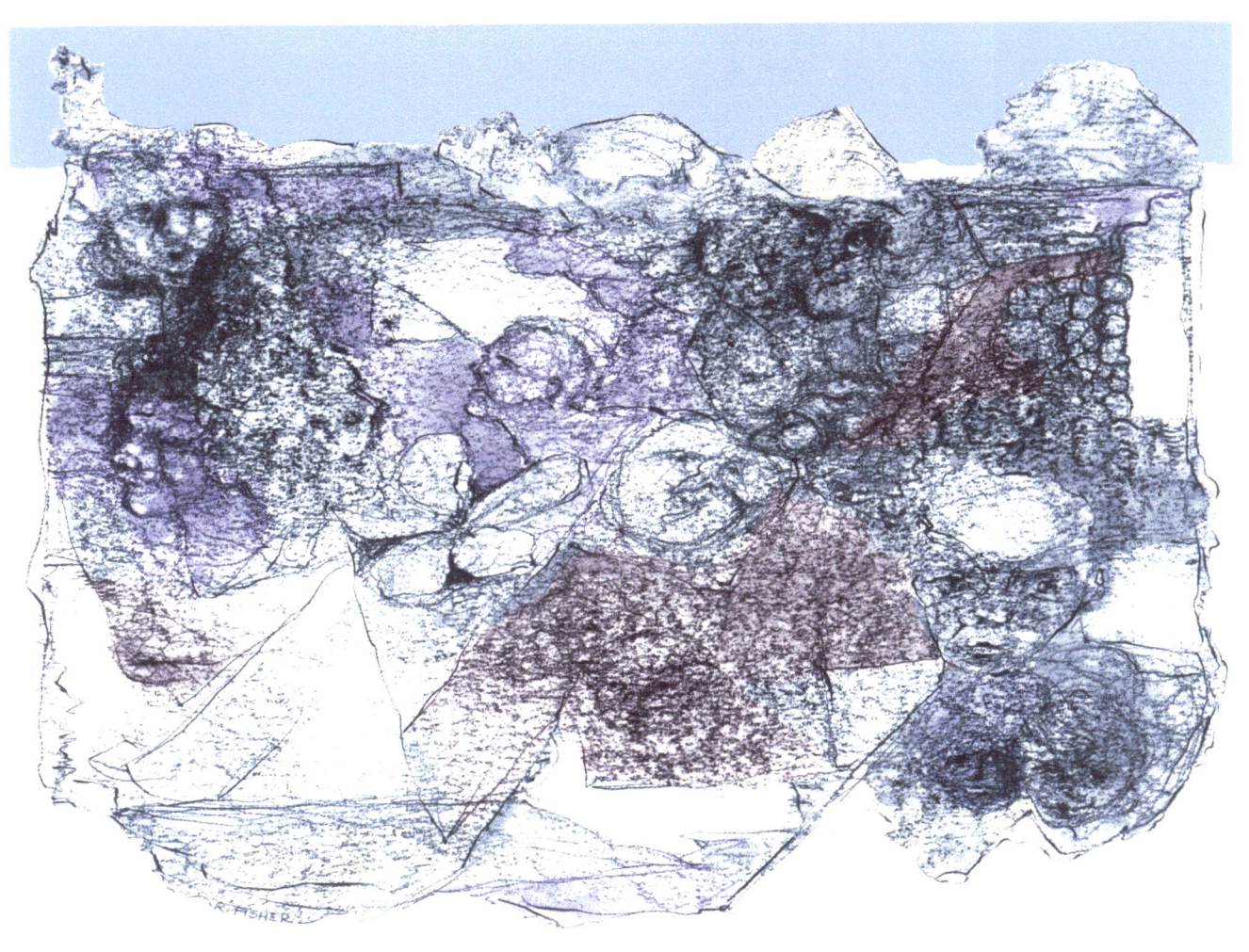

Indian River Lagoon

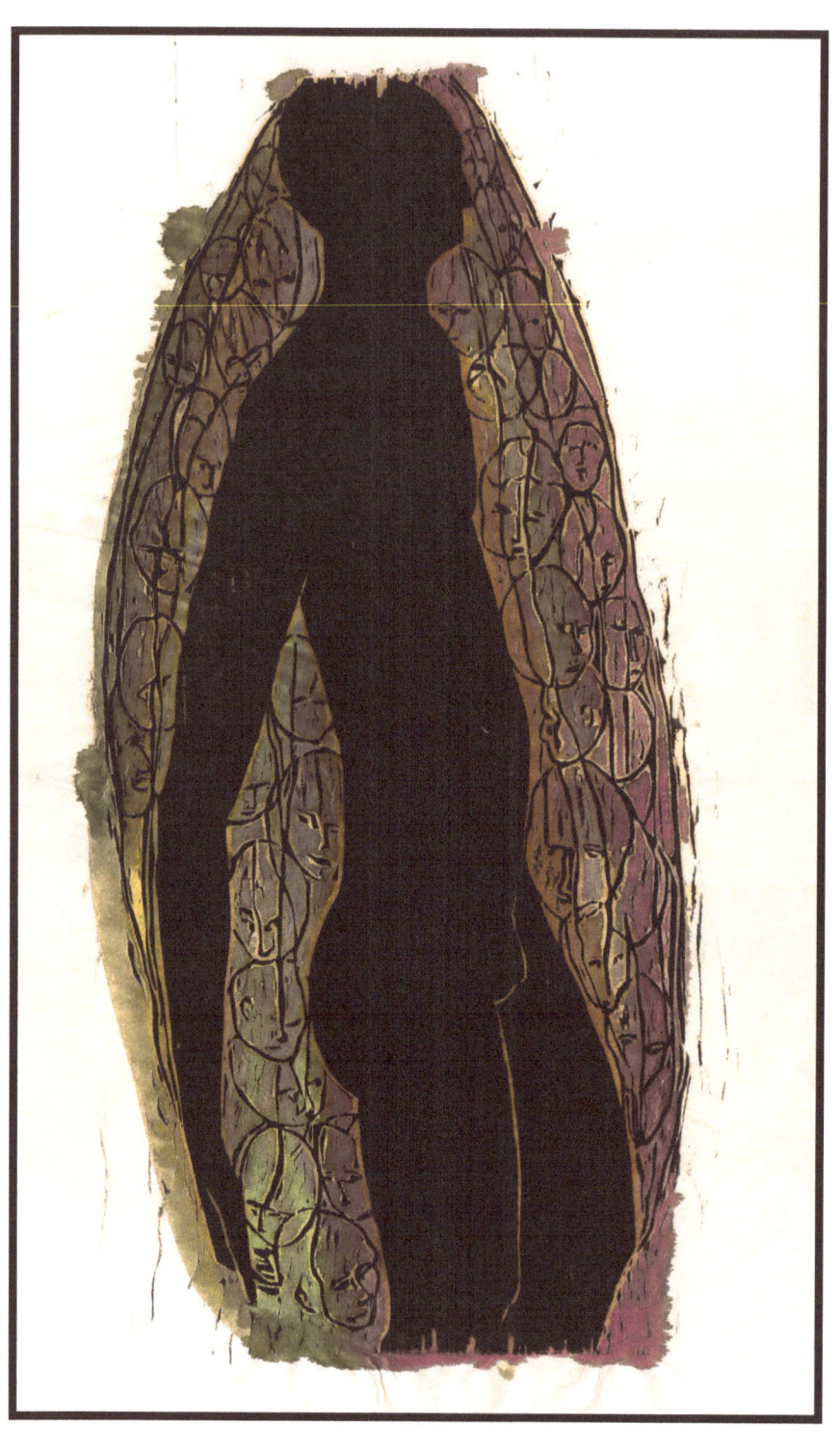

Image Gatherer
Wood Block Print

The original is a
wood
block print
enhanced with
watercolors.

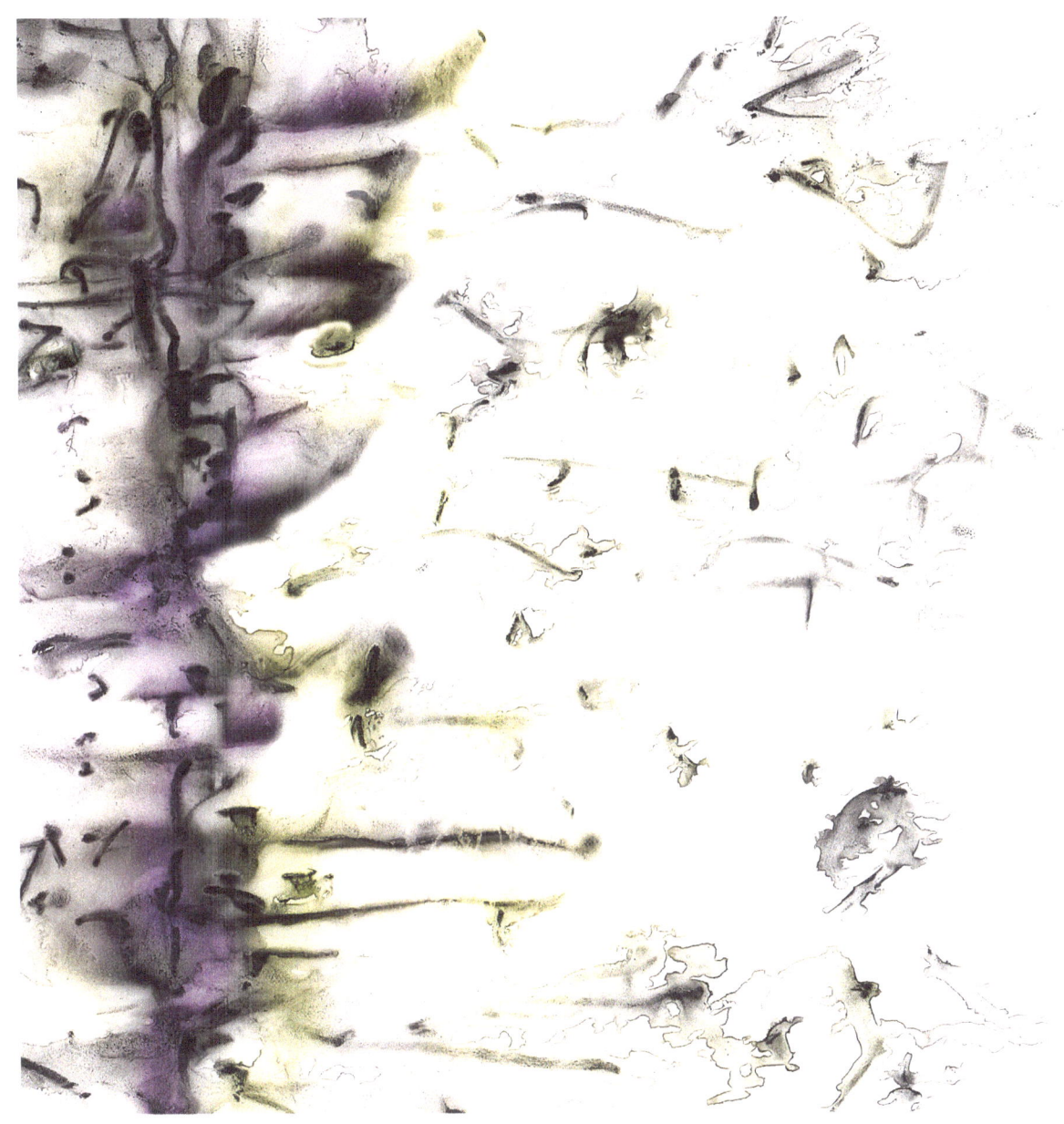

Judgment

"It is not in the stars to hold our destiny
but in ourselves." ~SHAKESPEARE

33

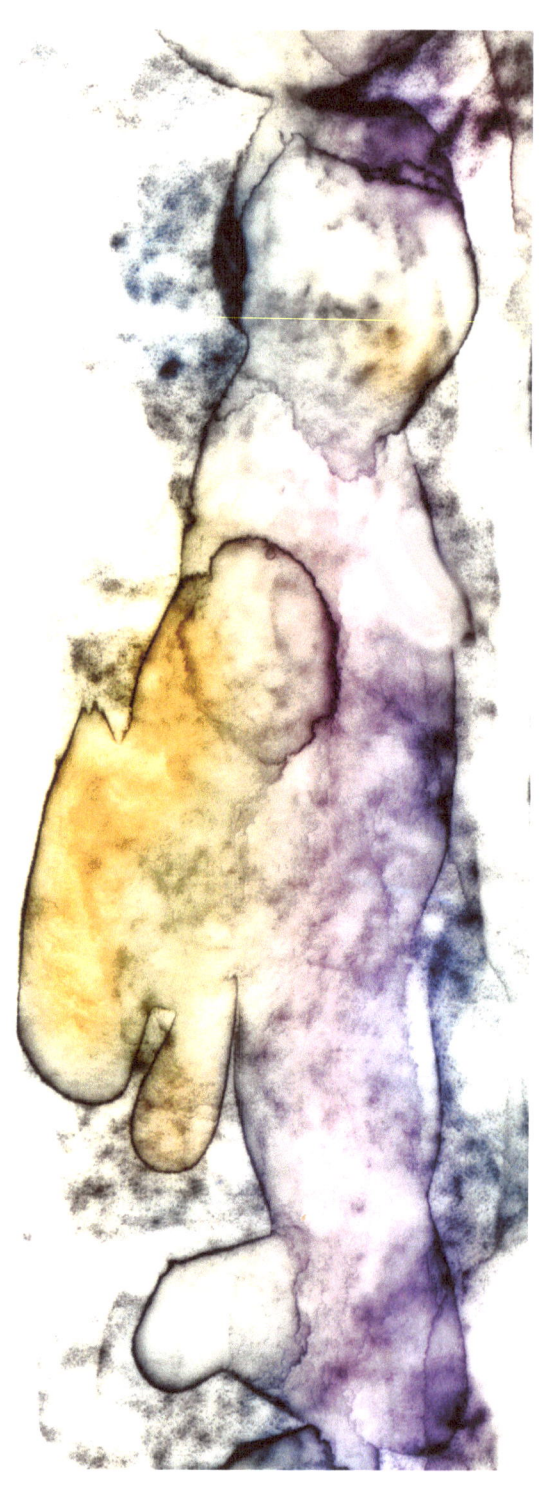

Mother and Infant

"We are always on a
jouney from darkness
into light. Your birth
was a first journey from
darkness into light. All
your life, your mind
lives within the
darkness of your body.
Each day is a journey.
We come out of the
night into the day."
~JOHN O'DONOHUE,
*Anam Cara, a Book of Celtic
Wisdom*, 1997

Gatherer 8e

"To be still is to be
conscious without
thought."
ECKHART TOLLE,
Stillness Speaks, 2003

Eros 3

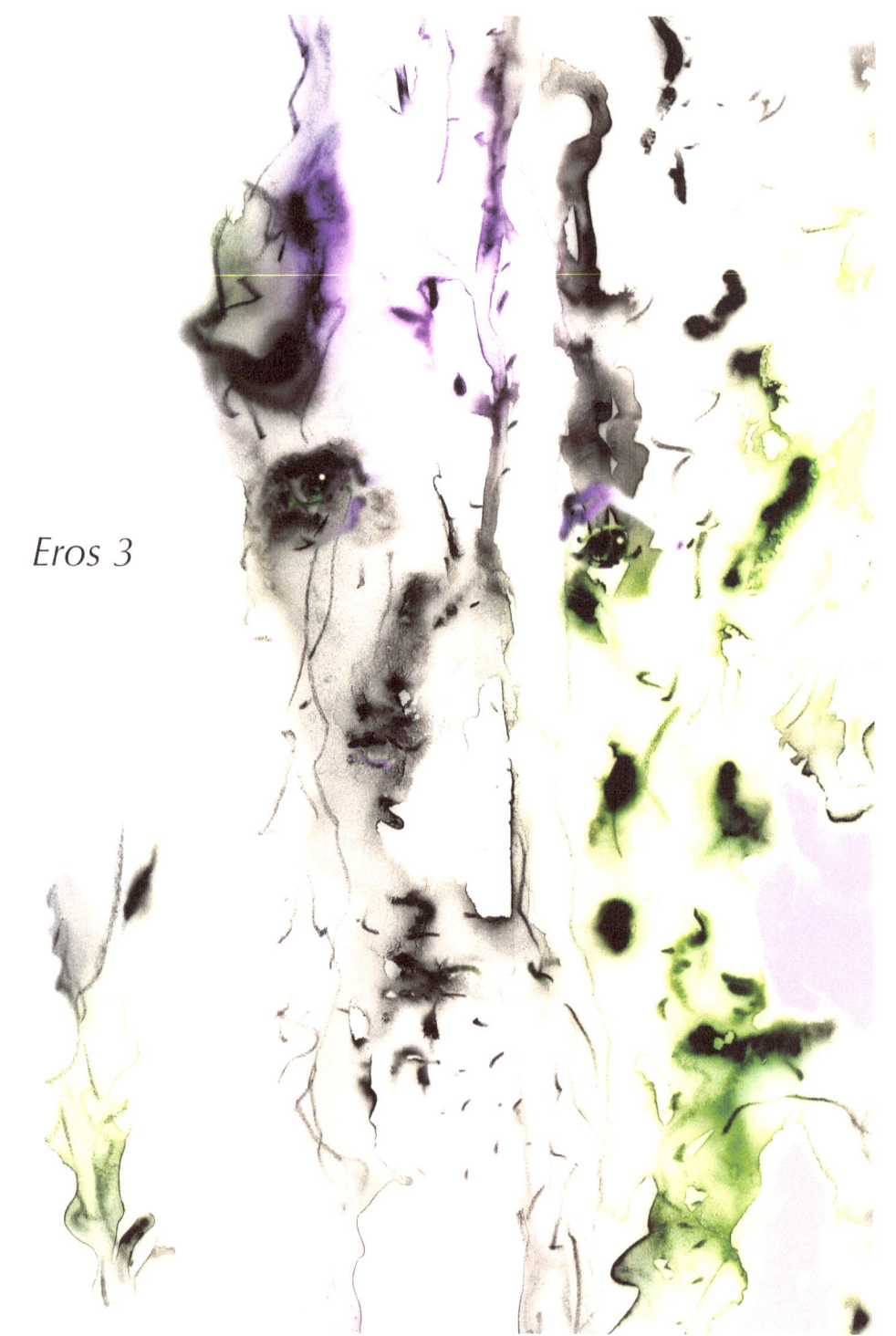

Samson

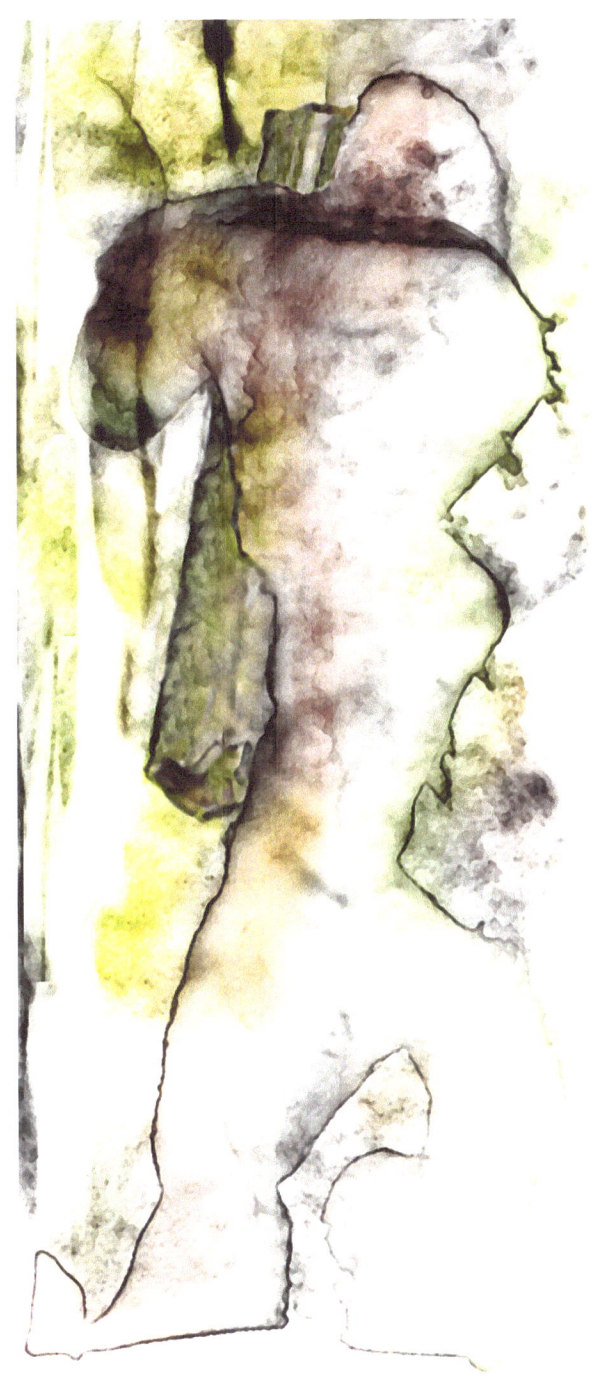

"The unconscious is a powerful and continuous presence. Every life lives out of and struggtles with this inner night, which casts its challenging and fecund shadow over everything we do and think and feel. When the unconscious becomes illuminated, its darker forces no longer hold us prisoner."
~JOHN O'DONOHUE, *Anam Cara, a Book of Celtic Wisdom*, 1997

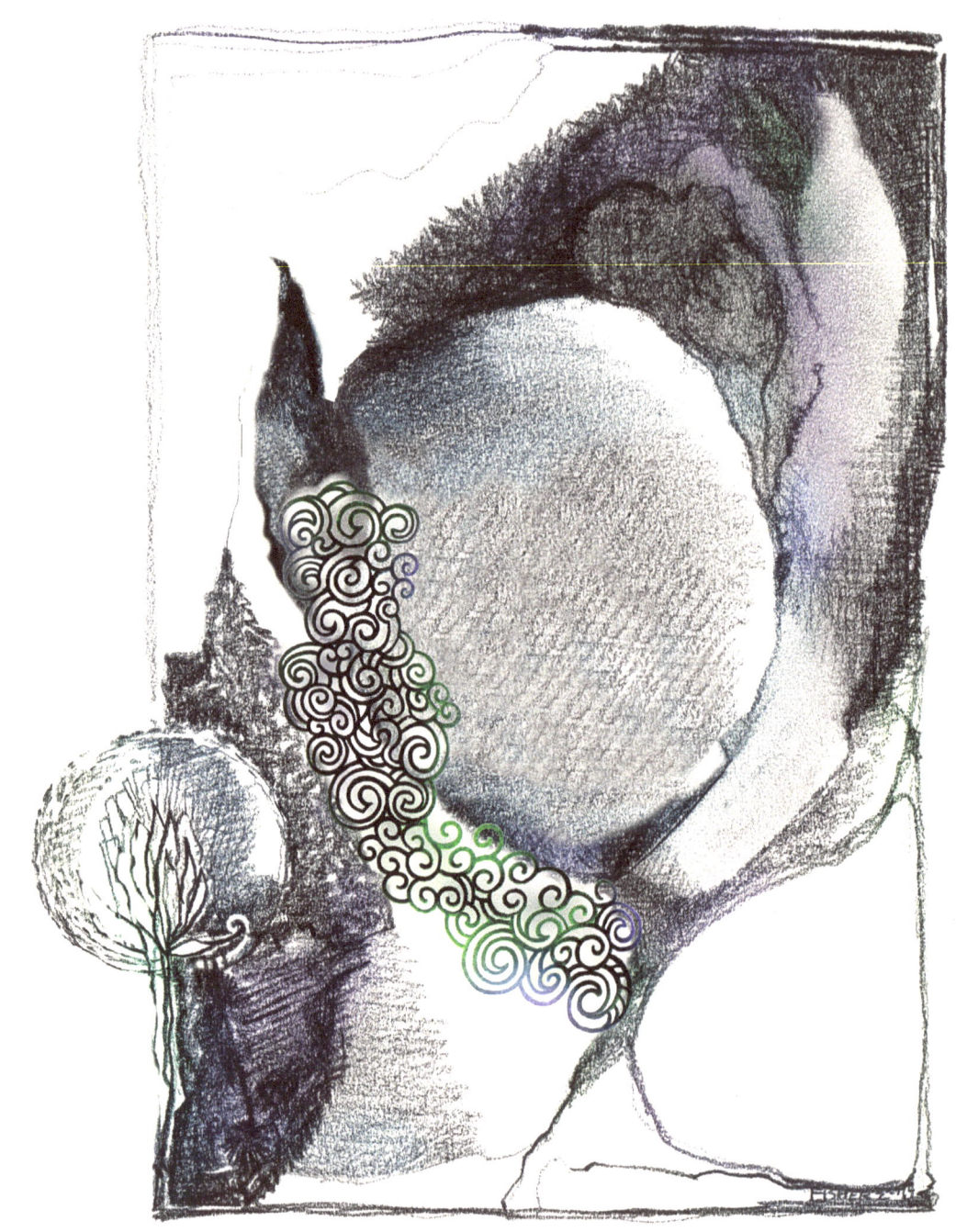

Mystery Flower

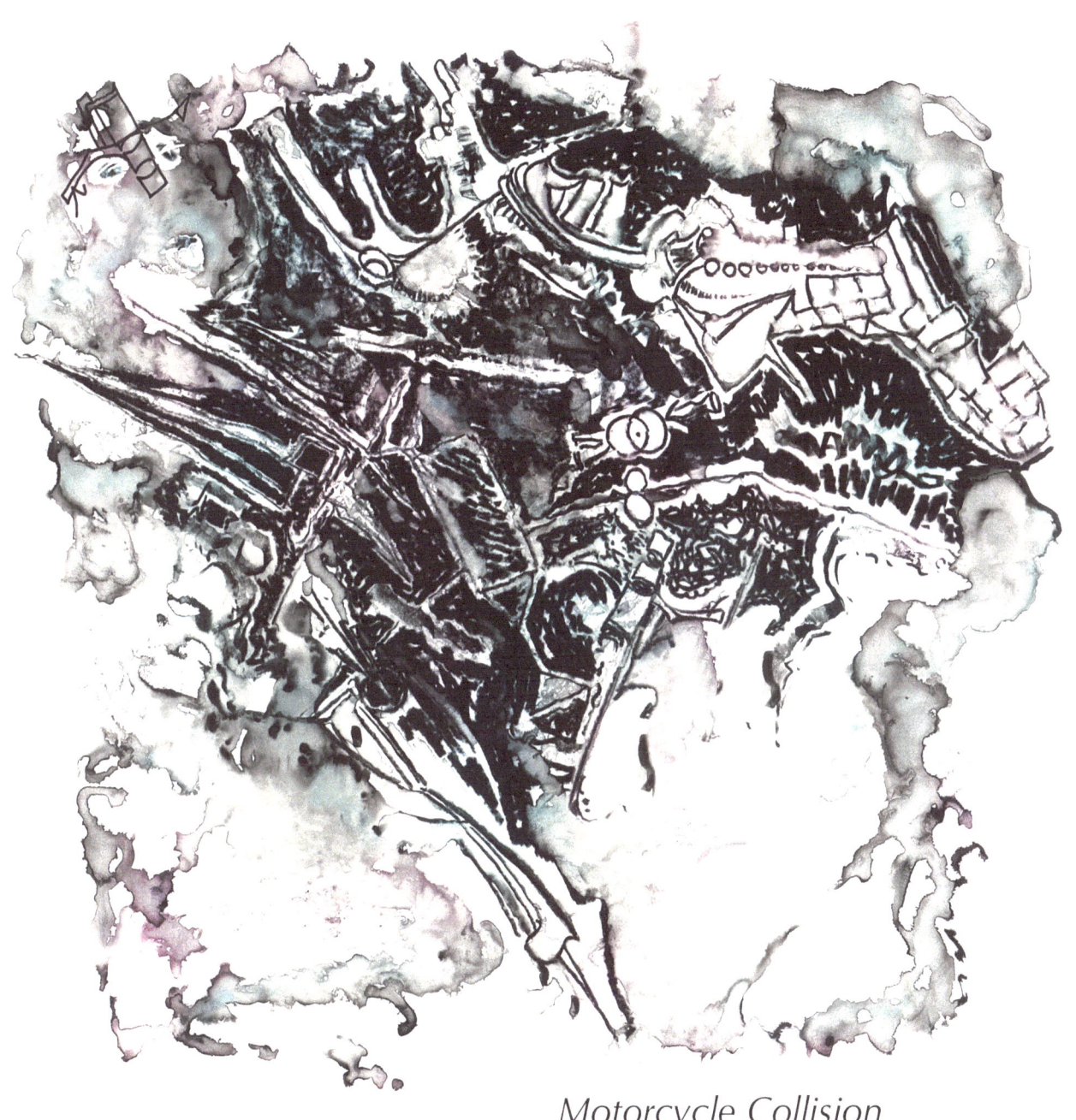

Motorcycle Collision

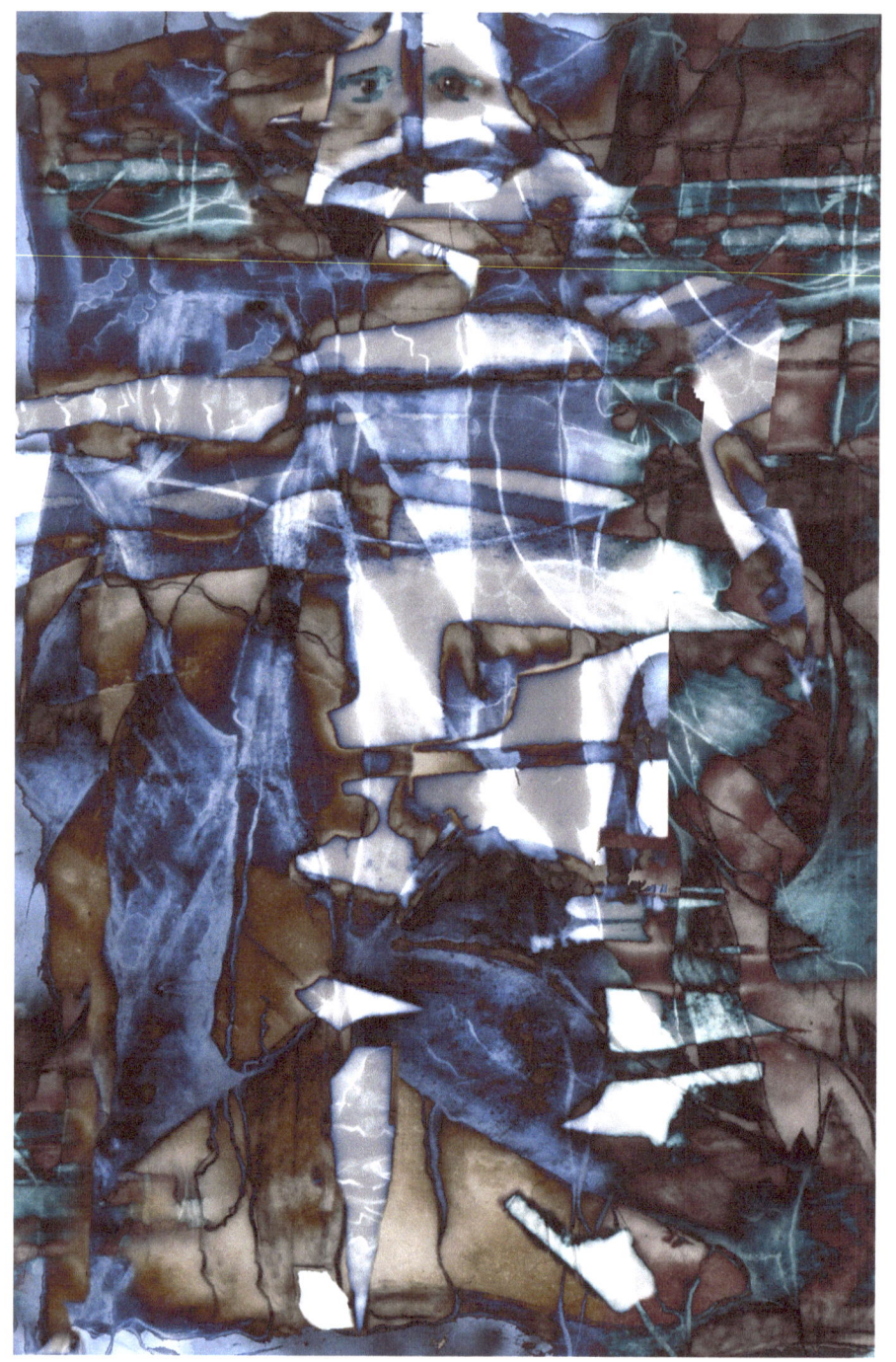

The Tin Man

"We hear he is a
wonderful Wiz
if ever a Wiz
there Was."
~from the film,
The Wizard of OZ

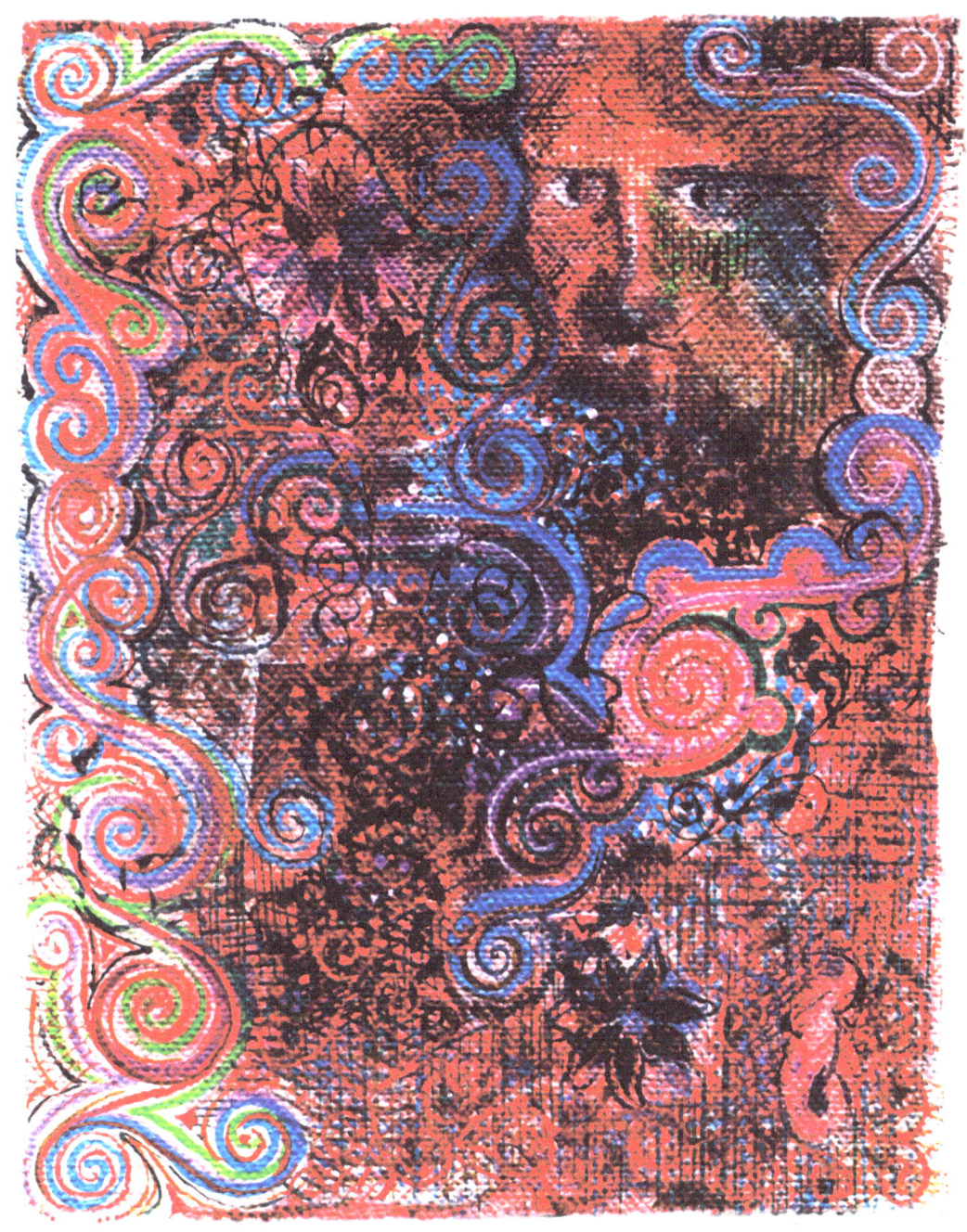

My Mind Maze

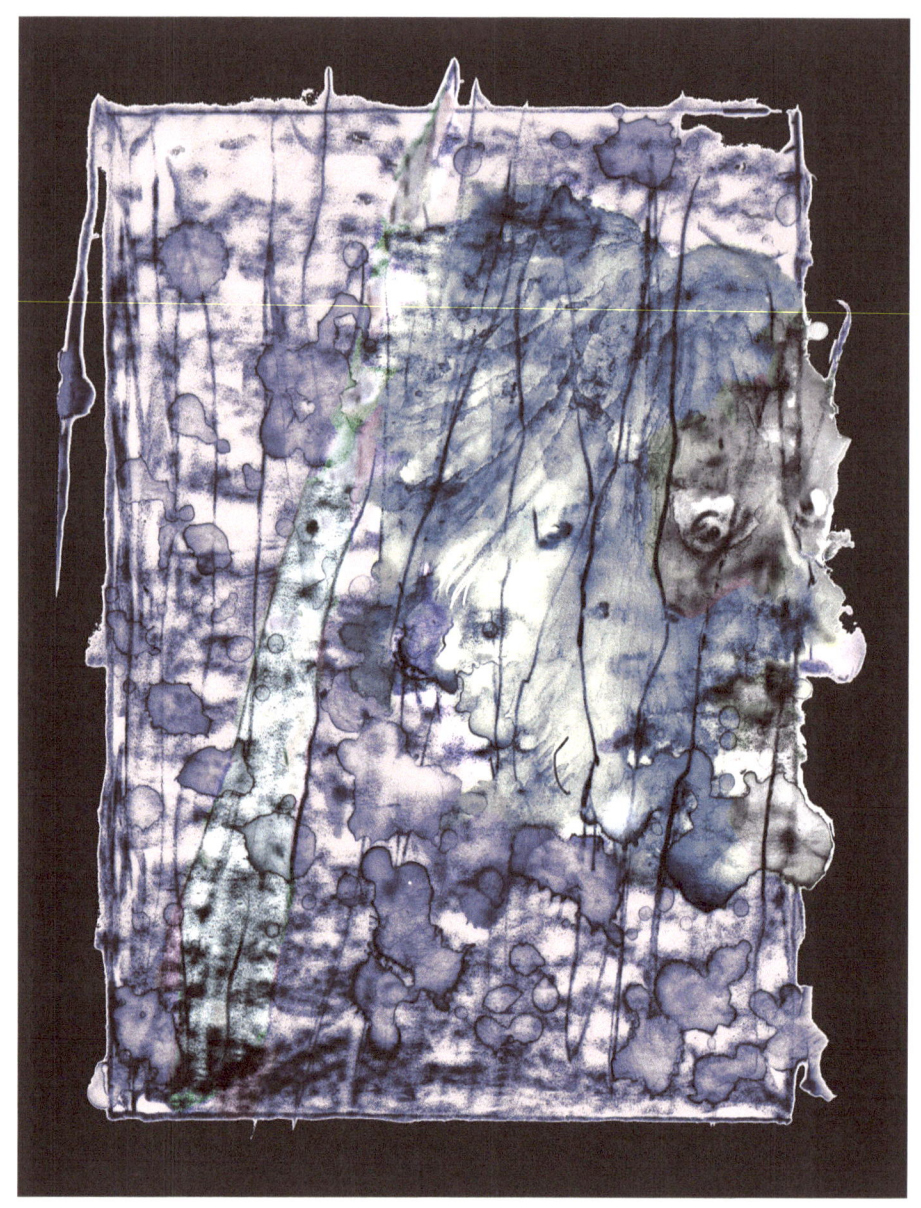

Damn! Angry Again
Artist's Proof

This is the first of several variations
of this image. Variation 3 is seen in
Volume 1 of MINDWORKS ART

Thinking Will Drive You

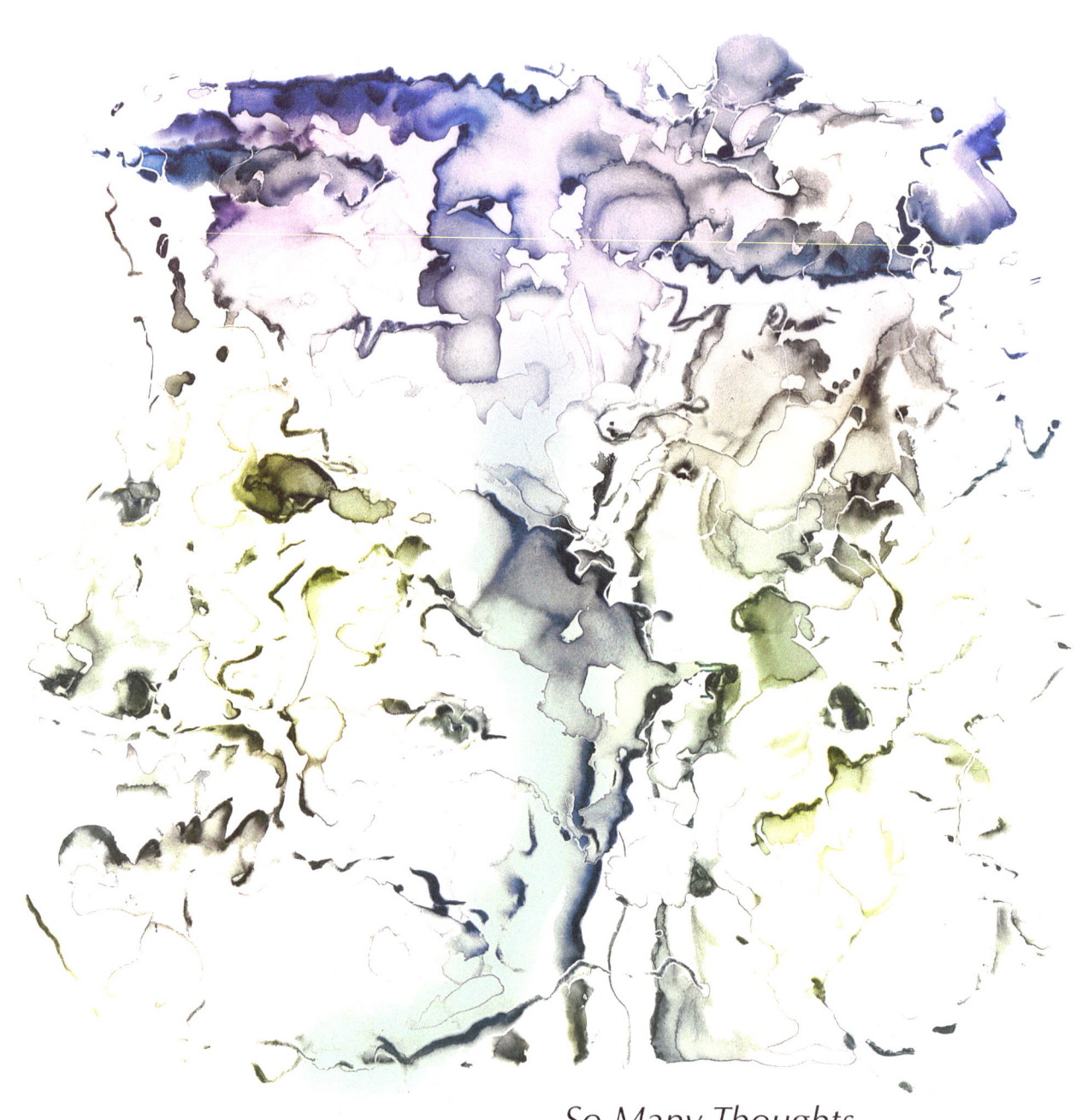

So Many Thoughts

44

Expanding

"Here is another way of finding inner space:
Become conscious of being conscious."
~ECKHART TOLLE, *A New Earth*, 2005

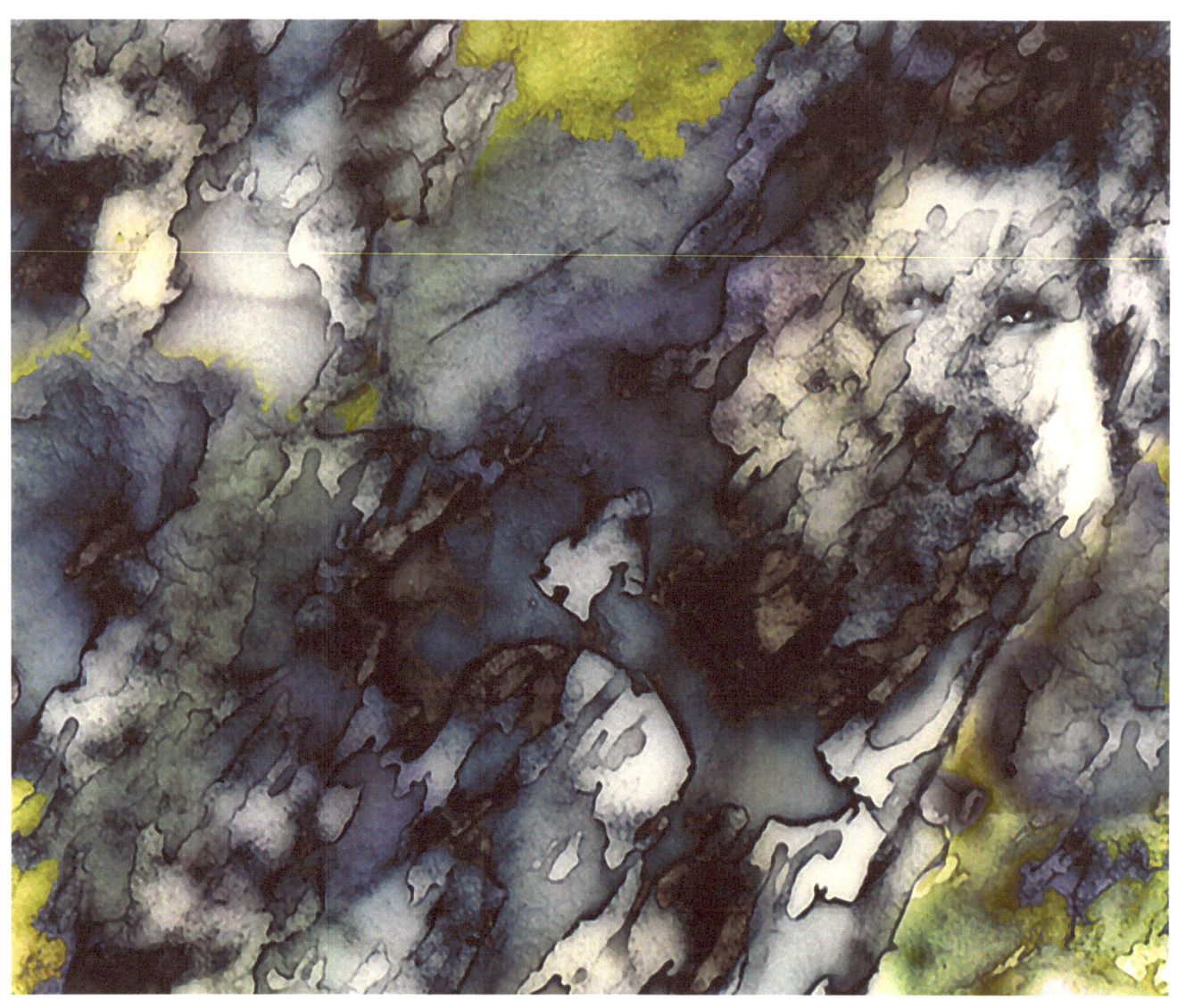

Depth Wandering

Mind Traveler

"Riddle of destiny,
who can show
What thy short visit
meant, or know
What thy errand
here below?"
~CHARLES LAMB
1775-1834

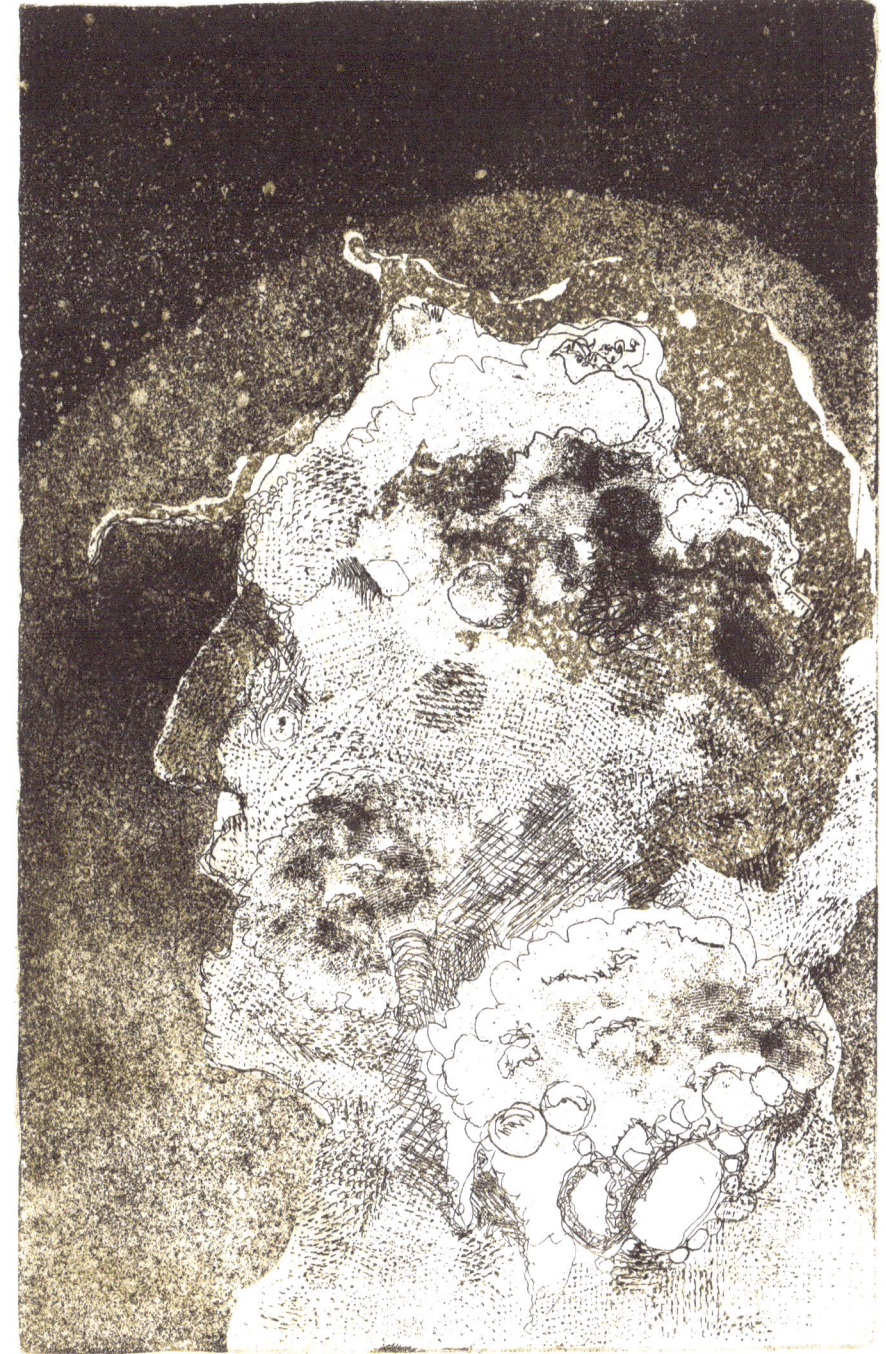

47

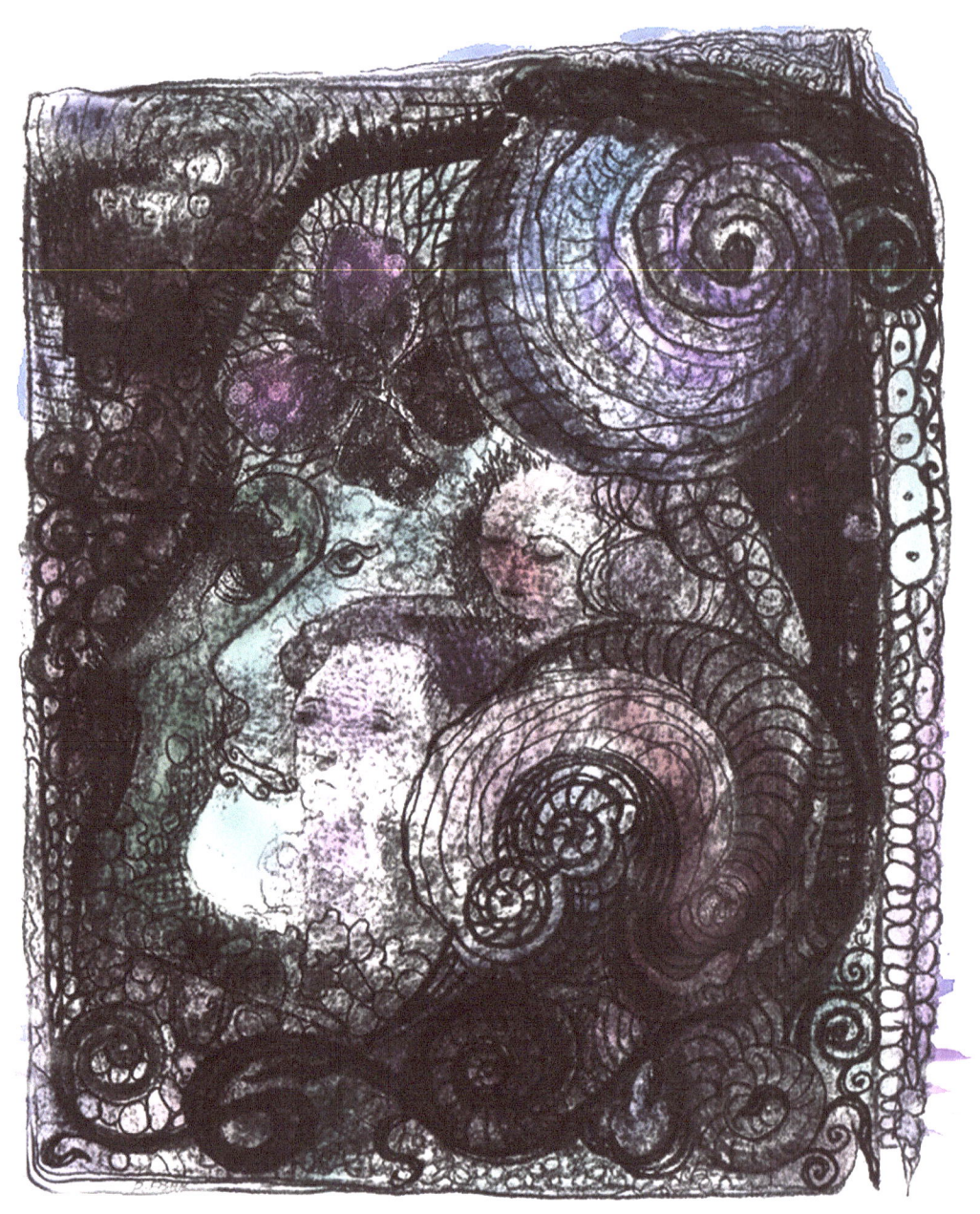

Ocean Beings

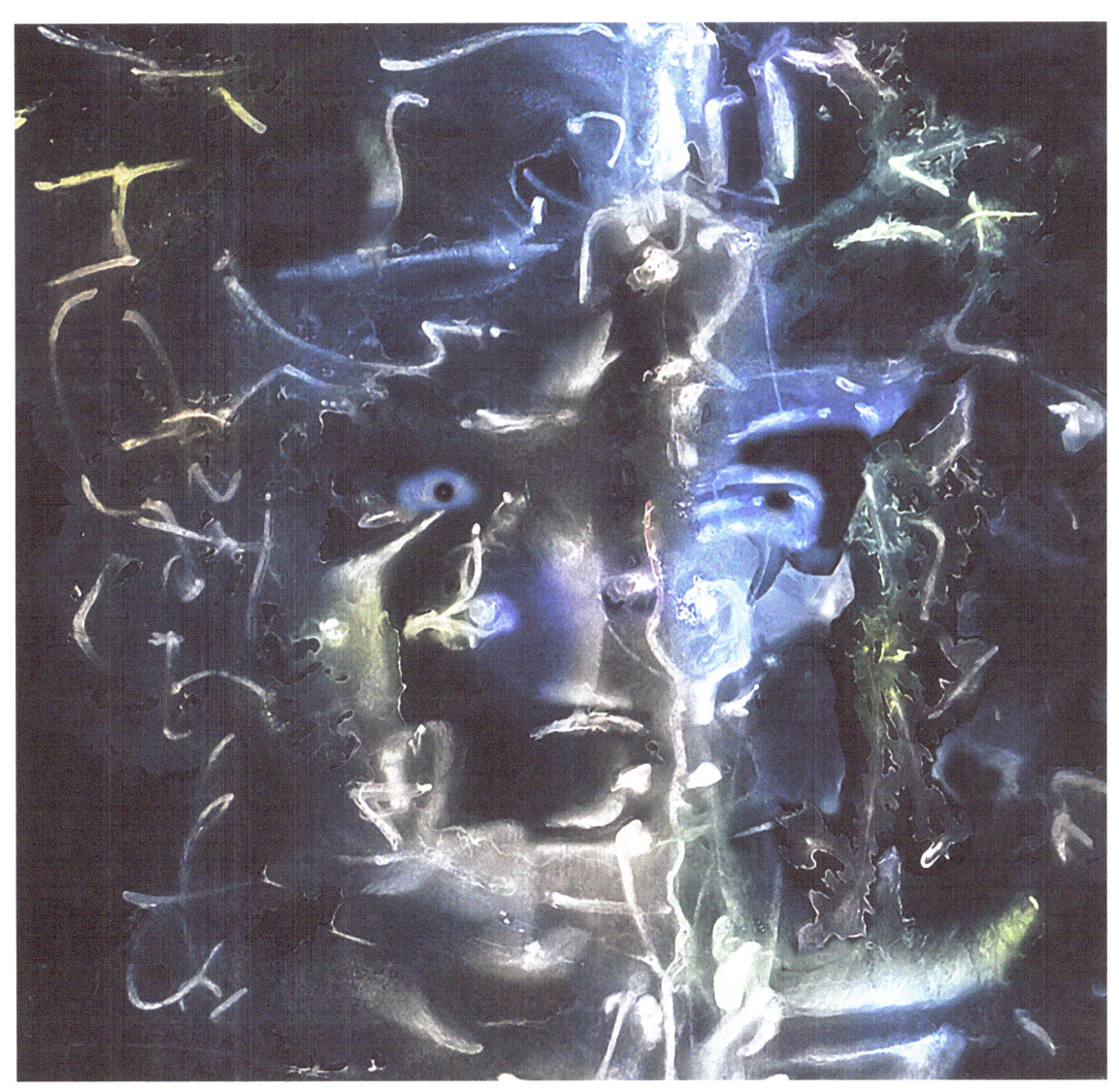

Night Caller

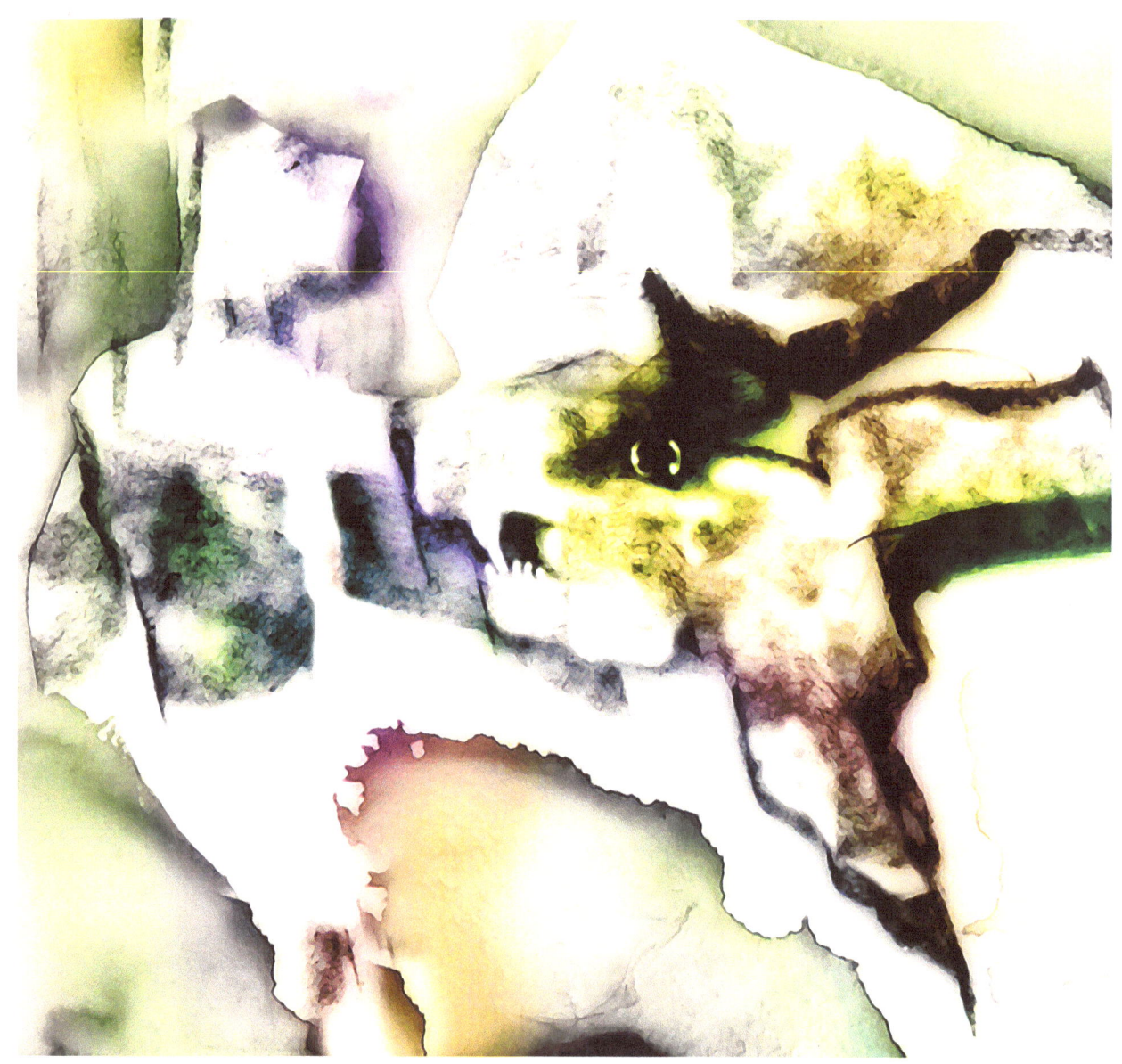

Man and Beast

"By the end of the (20th) century, the number of people who died a violent death at the hand of their fellow humans would rise to more than one hundred million." ~ECKHART TOLLE, *A New Earth*, 2005

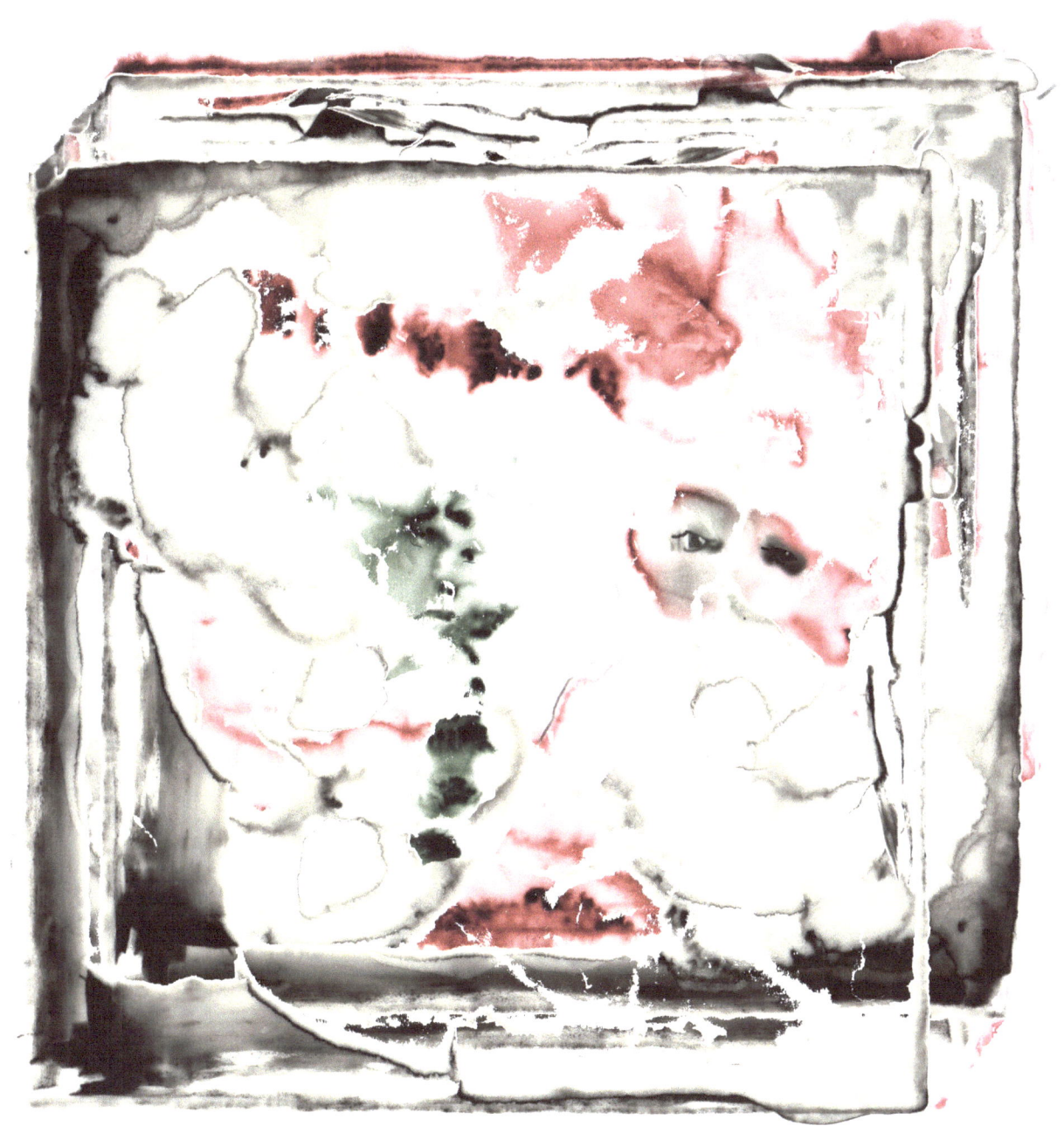

The Glass

51

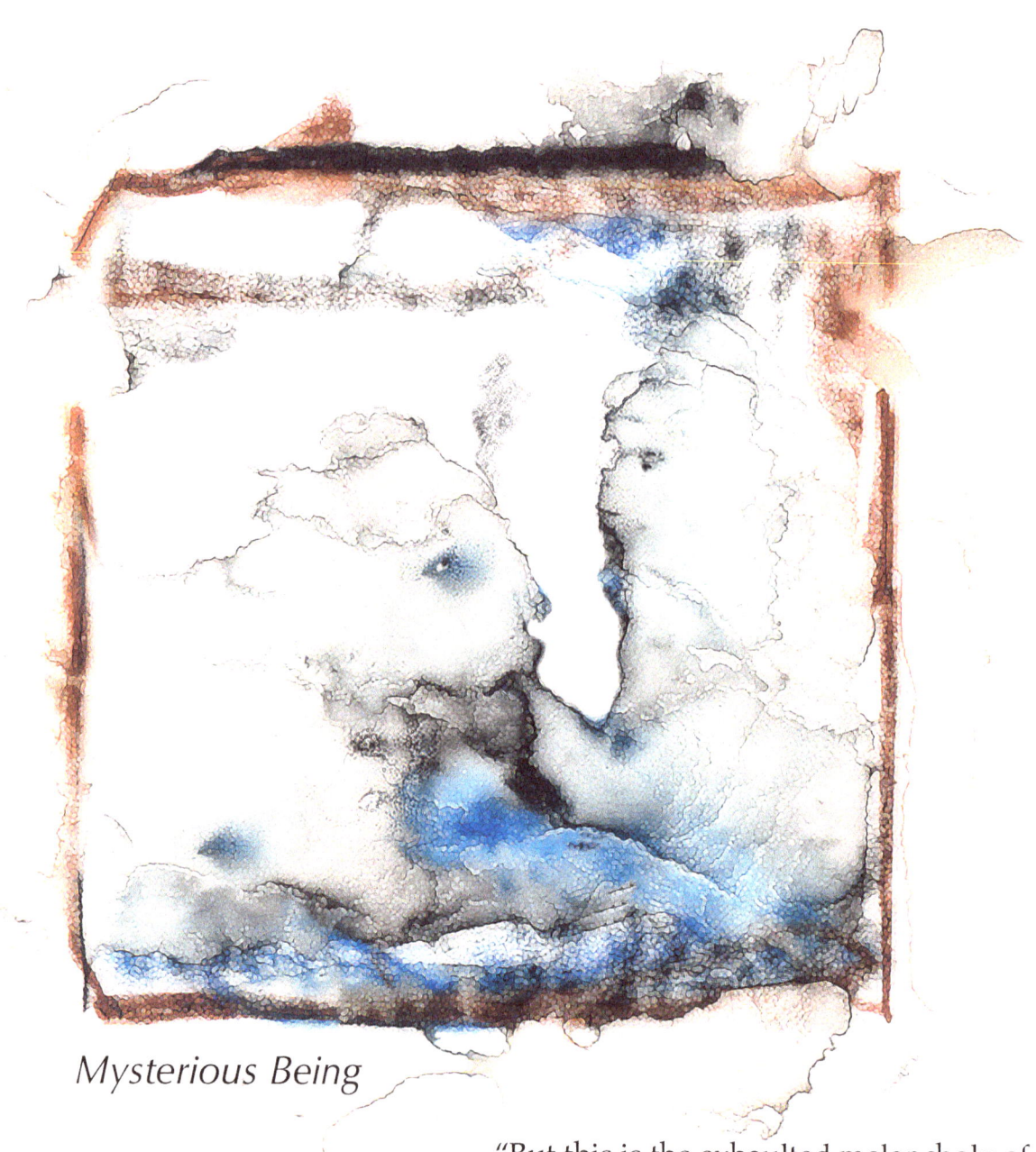

Mysterious Being

"But this is the exhaulted melancholy of
our fate, that every Thou in our world
must become an It."
~MARTIN BUBER, *I and Thou*, 1958

52

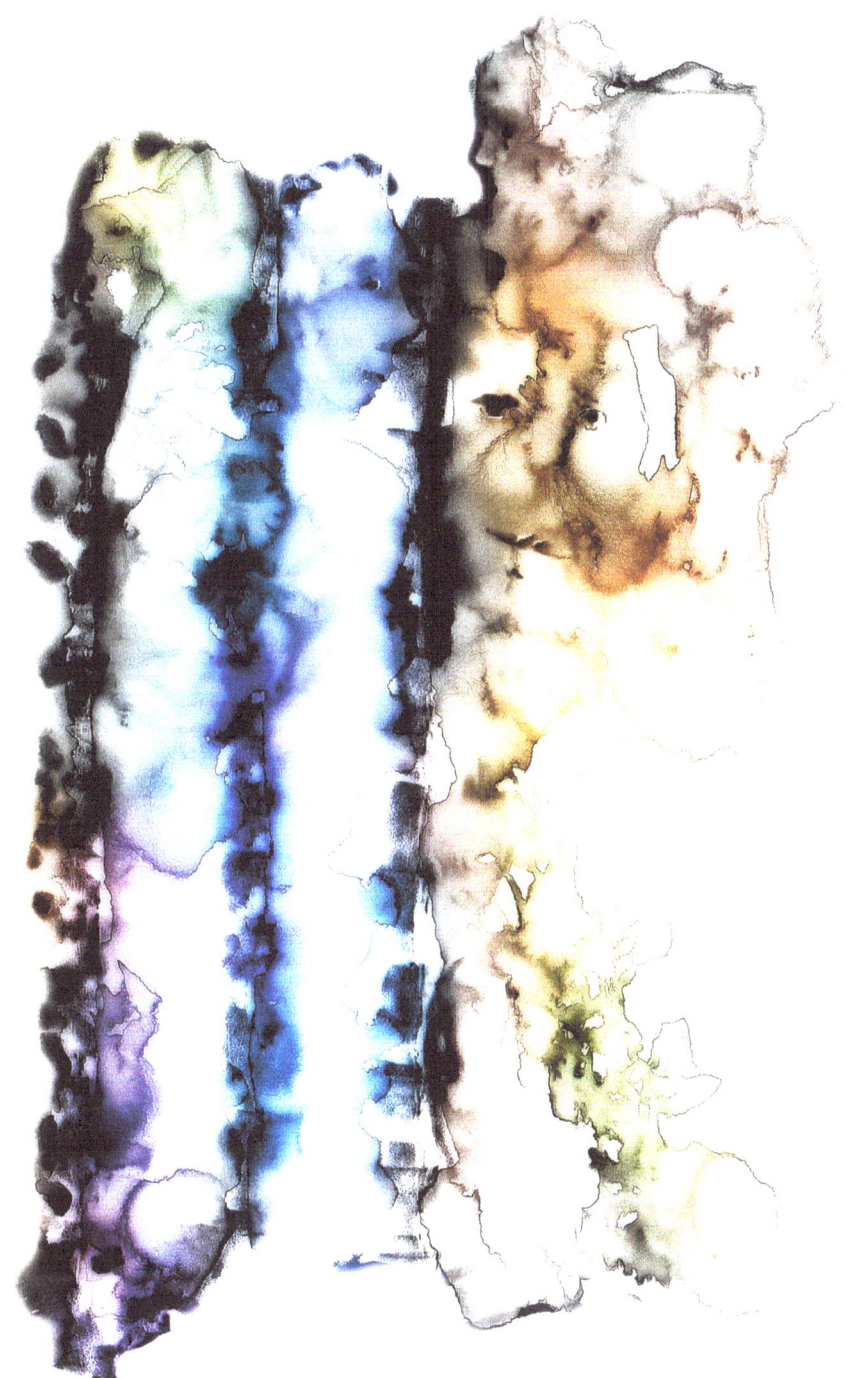

Us 'n Them

"An eye for an eye
makes the whole
world blind."
MAHATMA GANDI

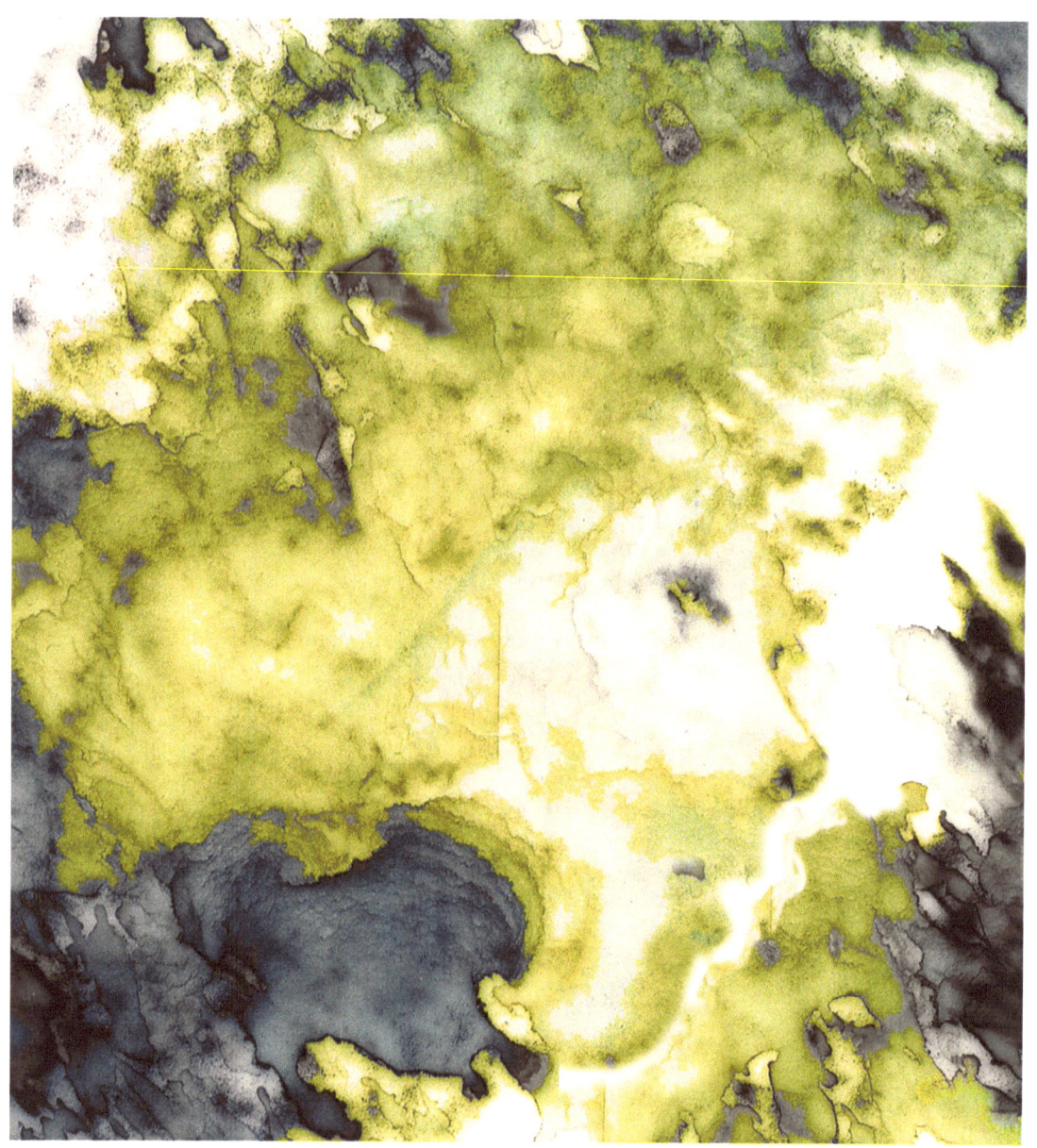

Golden Girl

"In all faces is shown the Face of faces, veiled
and in a riddle."
~NICHOLAS OF CUSA

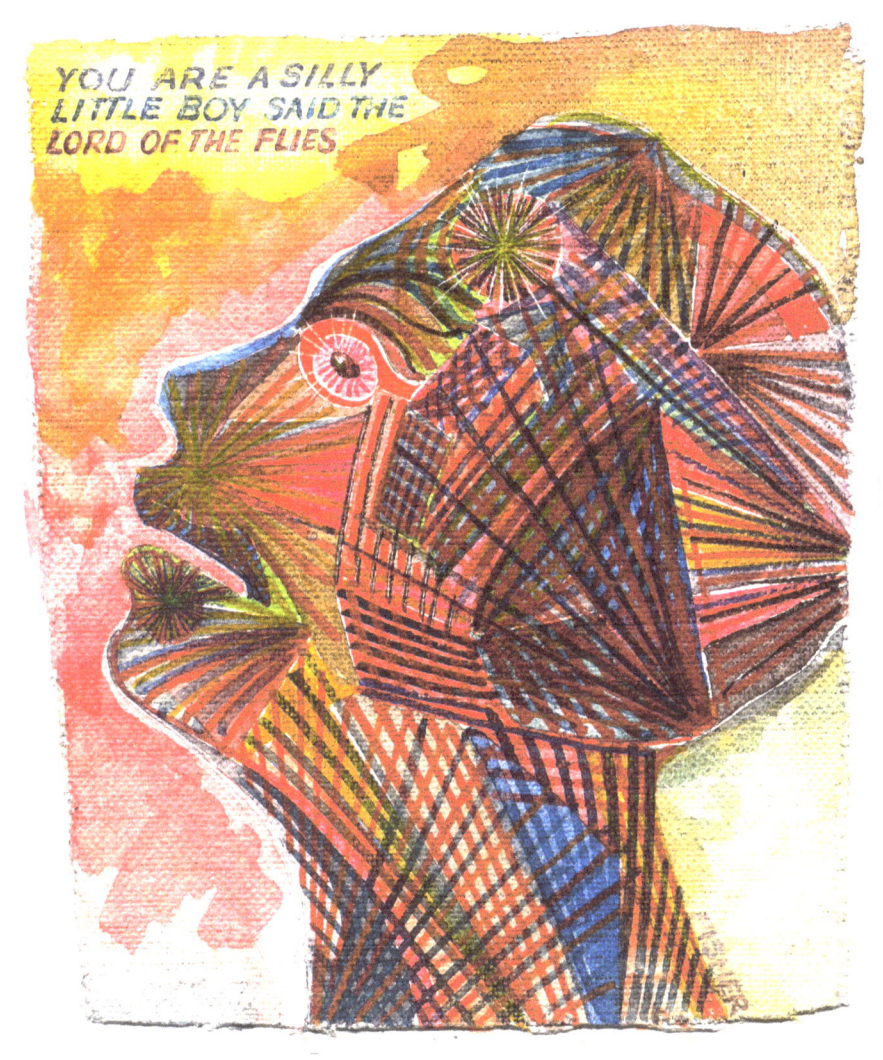

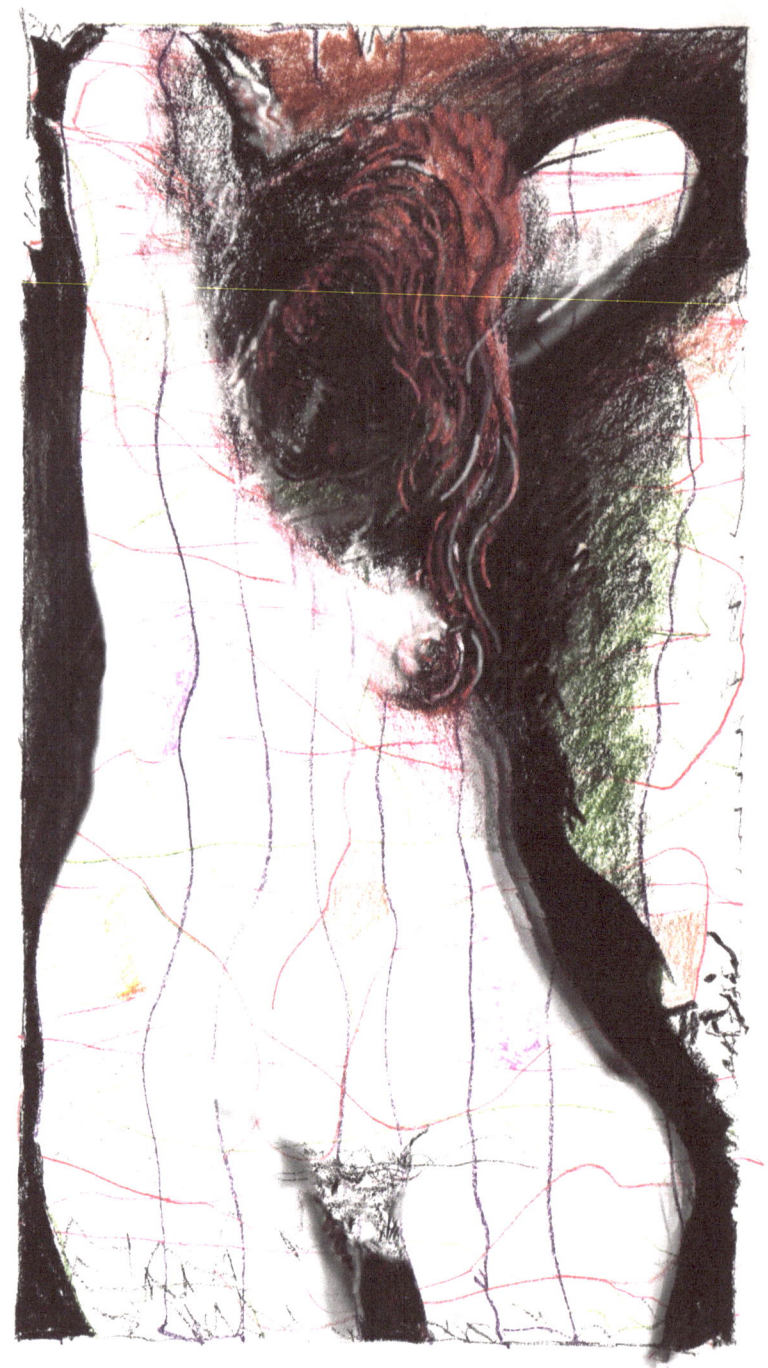

Woman

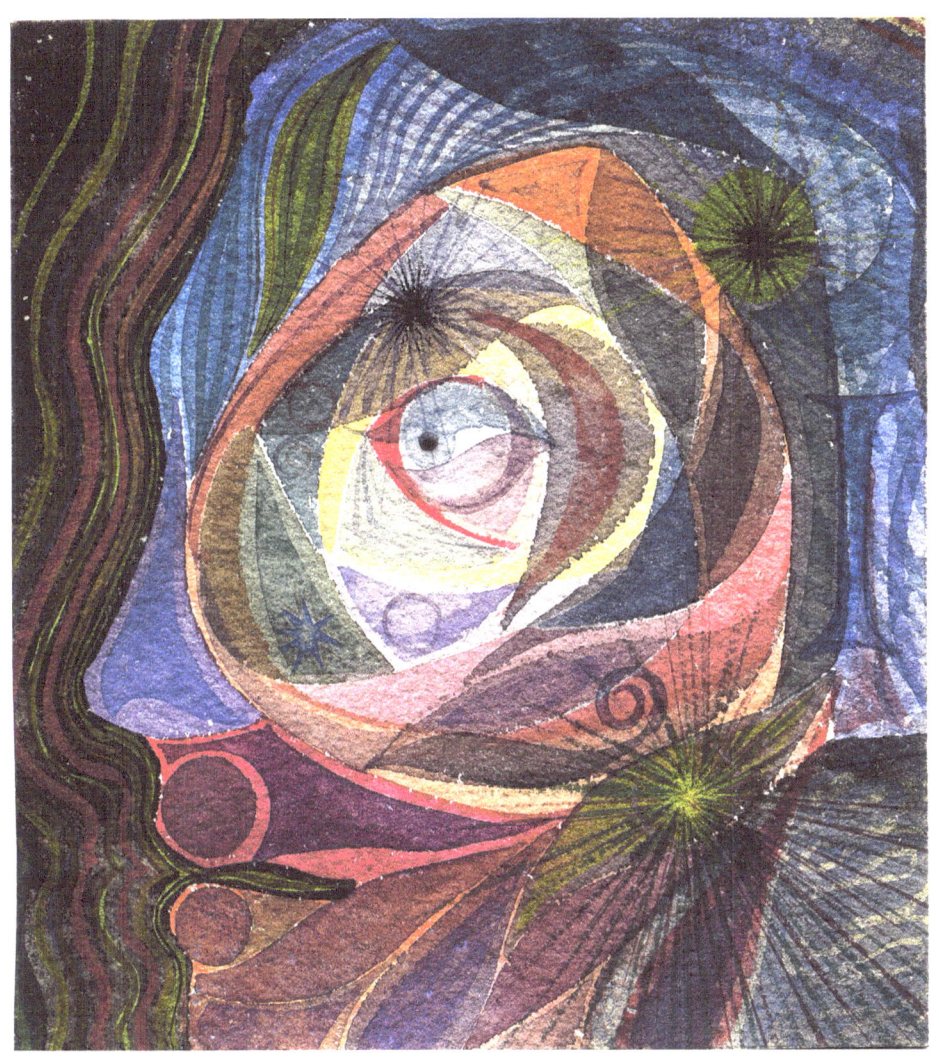

"I"

"I" ..embodies the primordial error, a "me" "my" "mine" and "myself" - a mis-perception of who you are, an Illusory sense of identity...the ego. ~ECKHART TOLLE, *A New Earth*, 2005

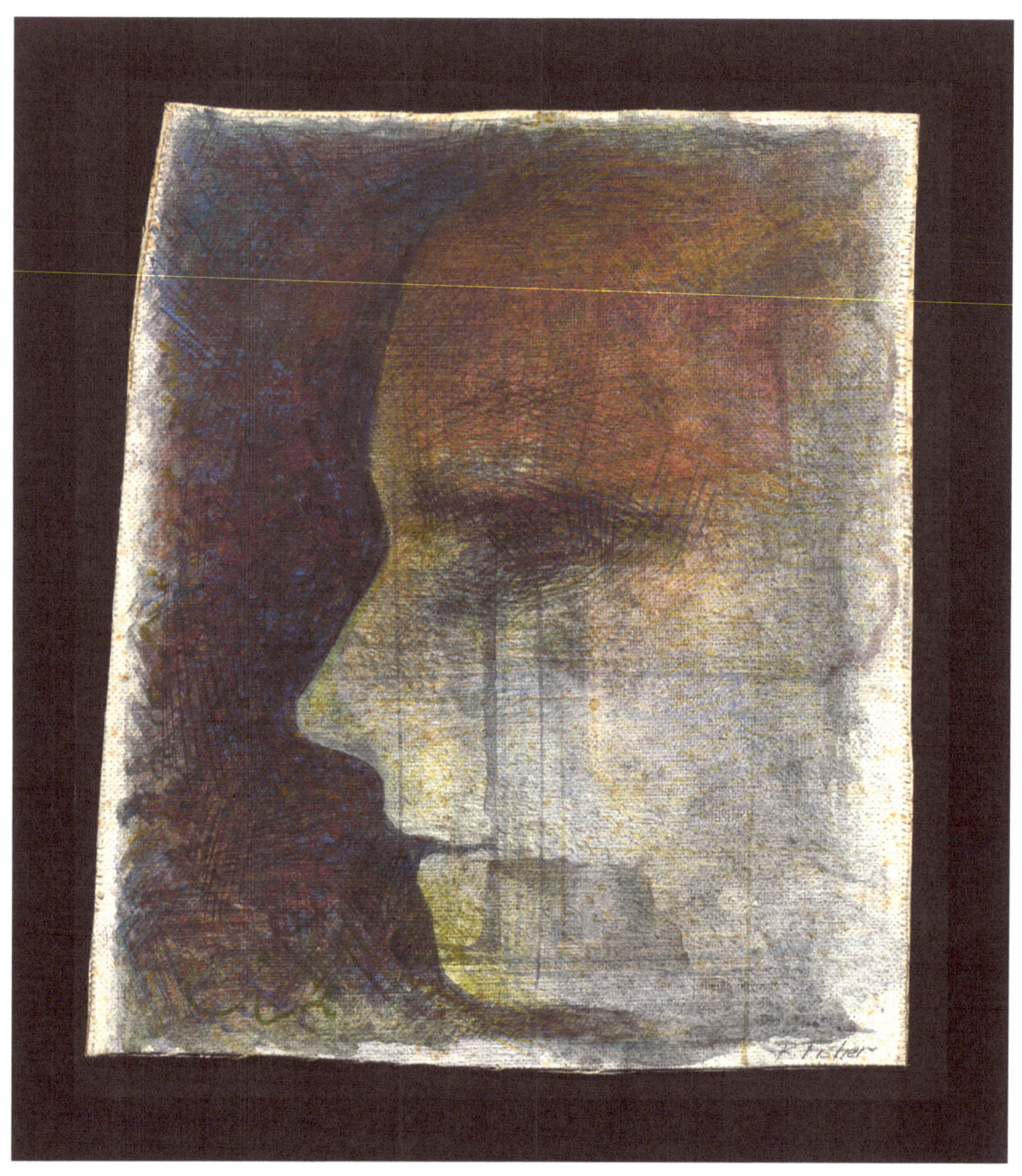

Soul of a Withered Man

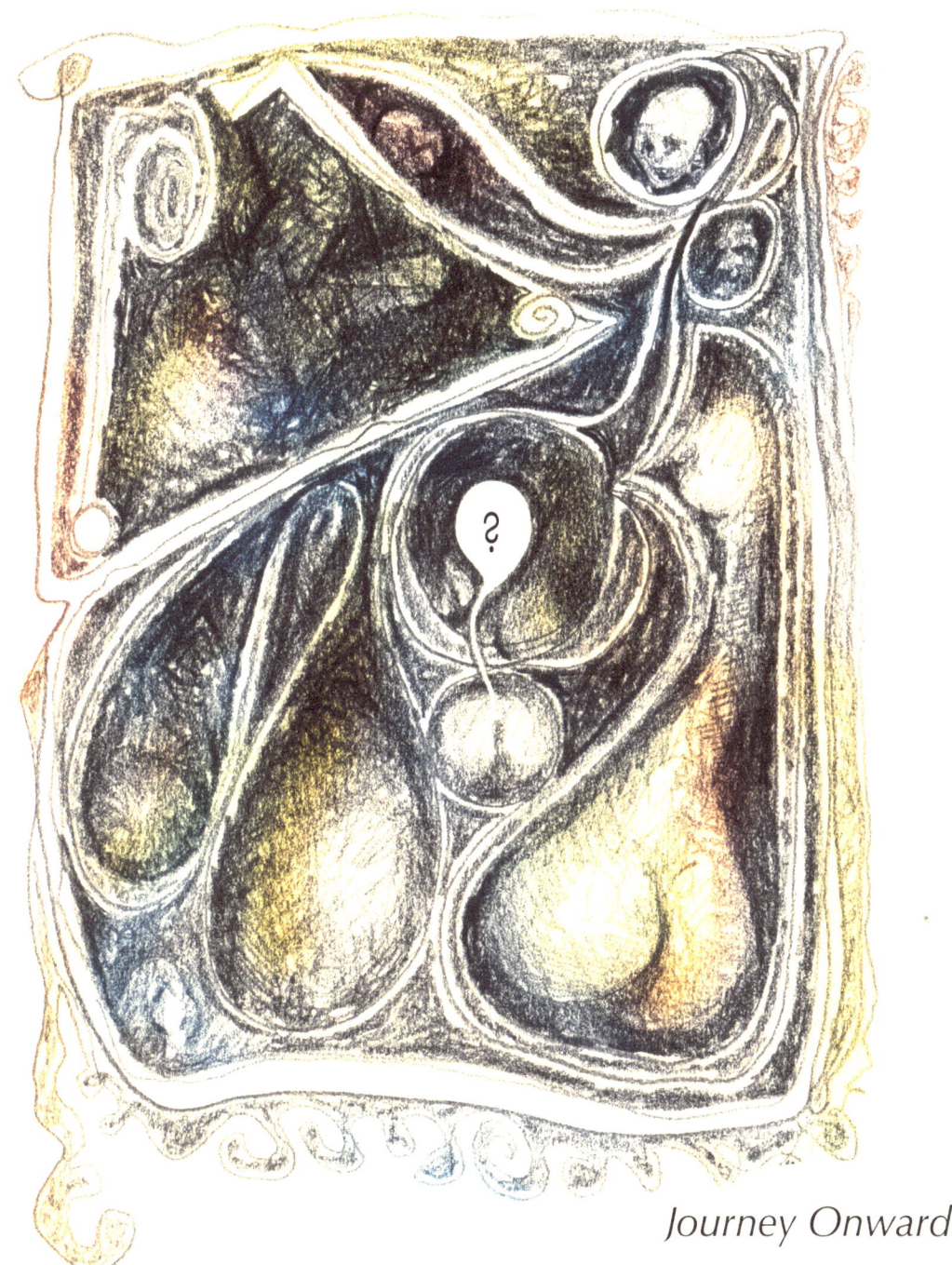

Journey Onward

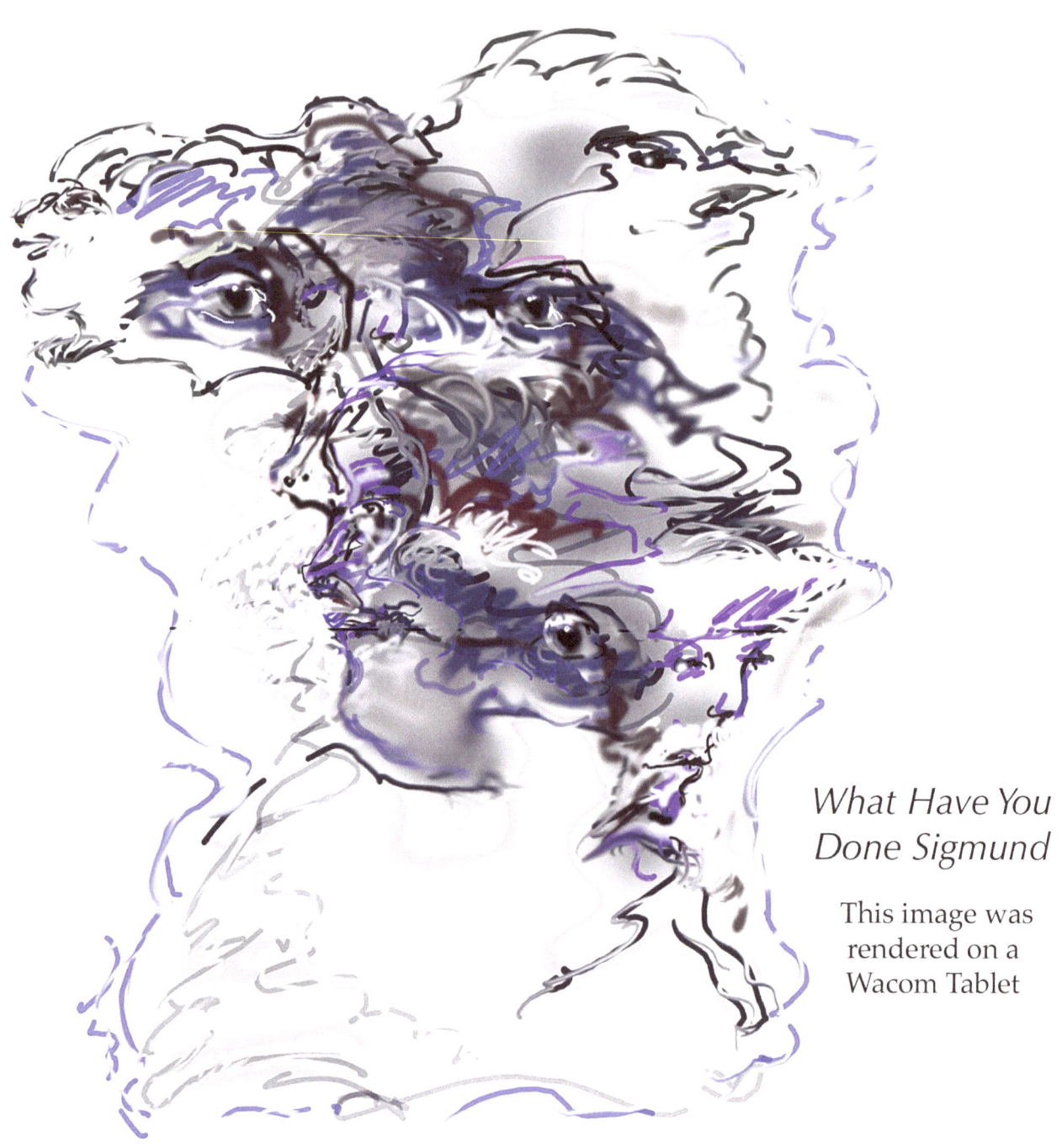

What Have You Done Sigmund

This image was rendered on a Wacom Tablet

A Brief Bio

Since the early 50s I have been continually involved with visual arts: BA degree from Pennsylvaniva State University, fine arts major; MA degree from Columbia University, Teachers' College, fine arts major; Parsons School of Design, advertising curriculum; Brooklyn Museum of Art, oil painting with Reuben Tam; extensive professonal experience in textile design, packaging design graphics, corporate identitiy programs, and finally teaching 22 years at the Fashion Institute of Technology (State Univeristy of New York) in New York City.

At FIT I taught textile (graphic) design from January 1975 to October 1997 in the Textile/Surface Design Department. Classes covered products from Home Furnishings to Apparel Fabric Prints; color fundamentals for beginning students; writing syllabi for advanced design classes in the upper division curriculum. The focus was on artistic skills, the current marketplace needs and the print technology necessary for industry. While at FIT, in collaboration with Dorothy Wolfthal, we wrote the department textbook: *Textile Print Design*, Fairchild Publications, 1987.

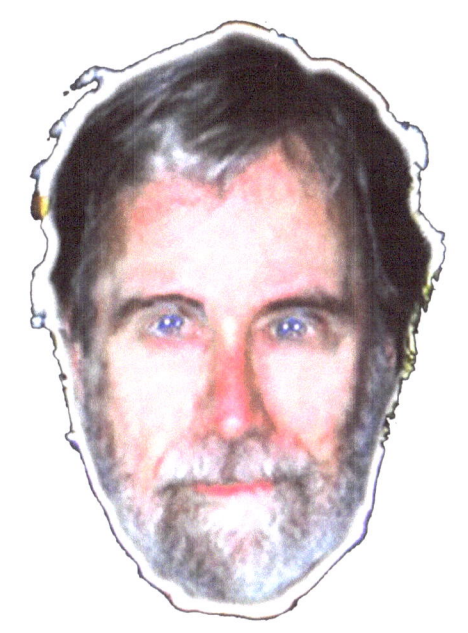

Richard

The advent of computer technology and digital art in the 1990s meshed nicely with the exploration of the unconscious mind which had begun for me in the early 1970s. In addition the new print technology allowed me to enlarge this imagery, making it more intimate and accessible to the viewer. The new tools of computer art opened 'doors of perception' as William Blake phrased it. It has been an adventure of discovery both artistically as well as spiritually, becoming more conscious in more ways.

Richard Fisher